AMAZING AIRMEN

AMAZING AIRMEN

CANADIAN FLYERS IN THE SECOND WORLD WAR

IAN DARLING

DUNDURN PRESS
TORONTO

Project Editor: Michael Carroll
Copy Editor: Cheryl Hawley
Design: Courtney Horner
Printer: Webcom

Library and Archives Canada Cataloguing in Publication

Darling, Ian, 1948-
        Amazing airmen : Canadian flyers in the Second World War / by Ian Darling.

Includes bibliographical references and index.
ISBN 978-1-55488-424-7

        1. World War, 1939-1945--Aerial operations, Canadian. 2. Canada. Royal Canadian Air Force--Biography. 3. Great Britain. Royal Air Force--Biography.
I. Title.

D792.C2D37 2009   940.54'4971
C2009-902464-0

1 2 3 4 5   13 12 11 10 09

Conseil des Arts du Canada   Canada Council for the Arts   Canadä   ONTARIO ARTS COUNCIL CONSEIL DES ARTS DE L'ONTARIO

We acknowledge the support of the **Canada Council for the Arts** and the **Ontario Arts Council** for our publishing program. We also acknowledge the financial support of the **Government of Canada** through the **Book Publishing Industry Development Program** and **The Association for the Export of Canadian Books**, and the **Government of Ontario** through the **Ontario Book Publishers Tax Credit program**, and the **Ontario Media Development Corporation**.

Care has been taken to trace the ownership of copyright material used in this book. The author and the publisher welcome any information enabling them to rectify any references or credits in subsequent editions.

J. Kirk Howard, President

Published by The Dundurn Group
Printed and bound in Canada.   www.dundurn.com

Dundurn Press	Gazelle Book Services Limited	Dundurn Press
3 Church Street, Suite 500	White Cross Mills	2250 Military Road
Toronto, Ontario, Canada	High Town, Lancaster, England	Tonawanda, NY
M5E 1M2	LA1 4XS	U.S.A. 14150

Mixed Sources
Product group from well-managed forests, and other controlled sources
www.fsc.org Cert no. SW-COC-002358
© 1996 Forest Stewardship Council
FSC

For Jane Ann

CONTENTS

Never, never, never believe any war will be smooth and easy, or that anyone who embarks on that strange voyage can measure the tides and hurricanes he will encounter.

— Winston Churchill, *My Early Life*

INTRODUCTION

With hindsight, I know exactly where and when I started this book. I was driving back to my newspaper in Kitchener at 4:30 p.m., November 11, 2002. I had just attended the funeral for my uncle, George Darling. He was a bomb-aimer on a Halifax bomber during the Second World War, and his pilot, Tom Lane, had delivered the eulogy.

As I drove on Highway 8, just outside of Kitchener, I realized that I didn't know much about what my uncle had done during the war. I knew he had been shot down somewhere in Europe and that he had been a prisoner of war, but I didn't know what happened to his bomber or what ordeals he had suffered. I decided to learn the details and write a story for my newspaper about him and his crew. I pieced the story together by reading his wartime diary and by interviewing Tom, as well as another member of the crew, Roy Macdonald. The *Record* printed the story a year later, a few days before Remembrance Day, 2003.

I thought I had finished writing about the war. Much to my surprise, I received phone calls and email messages encouraging me to write a book of similar stories. One such message came from Richard Rohmer, a Second World War pilot and a prolific writer. Apparently, I had erred in thinking that I had finished writing about the war.

That was six years ago. Since then, I have spoken to air force veterans who experienced horrific ordeals, and I have interviewed historians and archivists who provided additional information that I needed.

I hope this book is worthy of those who encouraged me to write it. Even more important, I hope it is worthy of the veterans whose stories appear in it.

Ian Darling
Kitchener, Ontario
March 2009

1
THE CAREER OFFICER

Keith Ogilvie wanted to join the Royal Canadian Air Force, but the air force turned him down. In the pre-war era it wanted university graduates. Ogilvie, who was twenty-four, was more athletic than academic. He had graduated from high school and worked as a clerk in an Ottawa stock brokers' office.

Ogilvie decided he would try to join another air force. In August 1939, he submitted his application at the Ottawa office of Britain's Royal Air Force. The office recruited him two days later, quickly gave him a medical exam and sent him to England on the ocean liner *Letitia*.

Within a month of Ogilvie's arrival the British government declared war on Germany. When he sent troops into Poland on September 1, 1939, Adolf Hitler demonstrated that he had no interest in what British Prime Minister Neville Chamberlain called "peace for our time." Hitler

The Ogilvie family

Keith Ogilvie about 1940.

wanted to use military force to expand German influence in Europe and around the world. Poland was the first country to fall. The Netherlands, Belgium, and France soon followed.

In September 1940, thousands of German troops assembled in France to invade the south coast of England. Hitler's invasion plan was called

Operation Sea Lion. The Germans lined up hundreds of river barges and other boats to take the troops across the English Channel. No invading force had come so close to England's shores since the Spanish Armada sailed into the English Channel in 1588.

Before Hitler could launch the invasion, Germany needed to control the skies over the Channel. The Luftwaffe had to defeat the RAF so that British aircraft could not attack the invading force.

The British people were grim and tense. The war had reduced the country's food supply, forcing the government to issue ration coupons for items such as bacon, butter, and sugar. Windows had to be completely covered at night to prevent any light from showing — light that could provide navigational assistance to German pilots. Great Britain was dark, literally and emotionally.

Though weaker than Germany, Britain was not defenceless. It could rely on Canada and other Commonwealth countries for assistance. It could call upon the Royal Navy's powerful armada to protect its shores. It had also strengthened its land forces in the south of England — the Home Office even released posters of German troops so the British people could easily identify enemy soldiers on their beaches, fields, and streets. Britain also had courageous men in the Royal Air Force, such as Keith Ogilvie, who by this time was a pilot officer ready to participate in the Battle of Britain.

Ogilvie belonged to the RAF's 609 Squadron, which was based at Middle Wallop, about one hundred kilometres southwest of London. The squadron flew the Spitfire, a single-seater fighter aircraft.

On September 7, 1940, the squadron was sent to attack several hundred German bombers and fighters flying toward London. From a distance, the planes looked like a cloud of hornets. Ogilvie felt excited. He was too busy getting his guns ready to feel frightened.

The Spitfires climbed above the bombers and positioned themselves so that the sun was behind them, becoming nearly invisible to German air crew. Ogilvie flew through the bombers, firing at one that had already been hit. The bomber started to go down, but Ogilvie lost sight of it because he was in the midst of the German formation. Trying to get out before a gunner fired at him he dove straight down, but he was too late. One of the gunners put a hole in the tail of his plane.

Ogilvie got away from the bombers and flew back up, getting ready to attack again. Just as he was about to swoop down, a Messerschmitt 109 — a German fighter — drifted in front of him. Then a second one appeared. The 109s were protecting the bombers, but the pilots didn't appear to see Ogilvie's Spitfire.

He fired, hitting the second one. It dove and turned over. He moved closer and fired again. Smoke and fire streamed from the 109. By then Ogilvie was out of ammunition, but he could claim to have destroyed the 109. Despite the hole in his Spitfire's tail, he flew back to Middle Wallop.

◆

Ogilvie flew again on September 15. His squadron was ordered into the air at 11:19 a.m. A controller told the pilots to look for bombers heading for Northolt, a few kilometres northwest of London. The sky was mainly clear with a few clouds.

Shortly after noon, 609 Squadron spotted about thirty German bombers over London flying at about 18,000 feet (5,400 metres). Fighter aircraft escorted them. The Spitfires tried to attack, but the attack failed because the German fighters fired cannon shells at them.

Ogilvie dove down and came up the side of the bombers. He saw some German fighters flying over him and felt thankful they hadn't come down to attack him. Then, in front of him he saw a lone aircraft that had become separated from the main formation, perhaps because it was already damaged. It was a Dornier 17, a thin, light bomber.

The Dornier released several bombs that were heading toward Buckingham Palace. Ogilvie fired at the bomber's port (left) side. The gunner on the Dornier fired at him. Ogilvie fired again. This time, the gunner didn't fire back. Ogilvie fired a third time. As he flew by, he could see a fire inside the Dornier's cockpit. Two members of the crew bailed out. The Dornier started to spin slowly. The tail snapped off, then the wings. The bomber was disintegrating.

Two heavy bombs from the Dornier hit Buckingham Palace. The following day the *Times of London* reported that one fell on the palace buildings and the other fell on a lawn. In addition, several small incendiary bombs fell on the palace grounds. These bombs started small fires that the palace staff and police extinguished.

Neither of the two heavy bombs exploded, the *Times* said. The one that struck the palace went through a private room used by Queen Elizabeth, who later became known as the Queen Mother. Neither the Queen, King George VI, nor their two children, Princess Elizabeth and Princess Margaret, were at the palace at the time.

The *Times* also reported that witnesses saw the bomber break into pieces. The wings fluttered in one direction; the fuselage dropped straight down.

This was the third time in a week that German aircraft had bombed the palace. The previous Friday, the King and Queen had been at the palace when six bombs dropped onto it. One exploded about thirty metres from the King.

———◆———

Wreckage from the Dornier came down in different parts of central London. A large section of the fuselage landed outside Victoria Station, scraping the thick walls of the train station.

The *Daily Mirror* reported that Londoners who were on Wilton Road near the station raced from the area as the bomber fell. It was the first bomber to come down in central London. The wreckage destroyed a jewellery store and damaged the station restaurant, trapping fifty women in the basement. The women had sought shelter there during the air raid. They didn't panic. Many had been knitting and, despite the intrusion of the bomber, they kept knitting. Their main concern, the newspaper reported, was that their lunch might be spoiled. Within a few minutes, some men rescued the women by prying open a door. "God bless our lads," one woman said as she came out, referring to the men in the RAF.

Another part of the Dornier landed outside a pub not far from Victoria Station, much to the joy of the pub's patrons.

The Dornier's pilot was Flying Officer Robert Zehbe. He bailed out of his aircraft and landed near the Oval, the cricket stadium in south London. Police took him to a hospital, but he died the next day. Two other members of his crew bailed out and survived. Two died on board.

After he had attacked the Dornier, Ogilvie flew back to his base, but he didn't stay there very long. His squadron flew again during the afternoon. At the end of the day, Ogilvie wrote that 609 Squadron had destroyed four Dorniers, probably destroyed another four, and had damaged several others.

Ogilvie had a successful, exhilarating day. He could prove he had fired at the Dornier because a camera synchronized with his Spitfire's eight machine guns recorded the attack. However, his exhilaration was tempered when he learned that one of his fellow flyers, Pilot Officer Geoff Gaunt, had been shot down. Gaunt was Ogilvie's roommate.

Although neither the King nor the Queen saw the battle above their palace on September 15, Queen Wilhelmina of the Netherlands did.

Queen Wilhelmina left the Netherlands on a British destroyer on May 13, 1940, a few days after German troops invaded her country. While in England she became a symbol of Dutch resistance to Nazi Germany.

Wilhelmina watched the battle from her London home. The fighter aircraft that shot down the German bomber impressed her. She asked one of her aides to write to the British Air Ministry to congratulate the pilot and his squadron. The ministry forwarded the queen's note to 609 Squadron, which gave it to Ogilvie.

The squadron's diary mentions the confusing nature of the battle over London that day, stating, "Who shot what seemed to be rather vague."

Considering the number of fighter pilots in the air, several could have attacked the Dornier bomber before Ogilvie.

One such pilot was Sergeant Ray Holmes, who flew a Hurricane with 504 Squadron. Holmes had been firing at several bombers when he approached one from behind. He thought the bomber was heading for Buckingham Palace. He pushed the firing button. Nothing happened; Holmes was out of ammunition. He made an instant decision to ram the bomber. He let a wing of his Hurricane hit the Dornier's tail fin. Part of the tail broke off.

The collision also damaged Holmes' plane. He bailed out, landed on a roof, slid off it, and ended up in a garbage bin. But Holmes was safe, and he returned to his base at Hendon in the northern part of London.

That very morning, Prime Minister Winston Churchill, who had taken over from Chamberlain, went to the headquarters of No. 11 Fighter Group in Uxbridge, a town just west of London. He wanted to see how the RAF fought German bombers that crossed the Channel. No. 11 Group covered southeast England.

In his book about the Second World War, *Their Finest Hour*, Churchill describes what he saw that day. The group's operations room was a small theatre, fifty feet (fifteen metres) underground. Churchill looked down on a large map of the south of England. About twenty men and women moved discs on the map that represented planes in the air. Information about the flight paths of German aircraft flowed from radar units and the Observer Corps. The observers were trained to look for enemy aircraft and to report what they saw. On one wall in the room a blackboard listed all the squadrons in No. 11 Group. Lights flashed on it to show the state that the squadrons were in. A red light meant the squadron was fighting the enemy.

When Churchill first entered the room, he didn't know whether he would see any raids plotted on the map. But during the morning, the plotters moved the discs a lot. The Luftwaffe was sending wave after wave of bombers. The lights showed that the RAF pilots were airborne — Pilot Officer Keith Ogilvie was one of them.

Churchill turned to Air Vice Marshal Keith Park, who directed the fighters, and asked, "What other reserves have we?" Park provided a straightforward answer: "There are none." The RAF had put every available fighter into the sky.

—————◆—————

Churchill found his experience at No. 11 Fighter Group's operations room to be exhausting. He returned to his home and slept. When he woke up, he asked about the day's battles. His secretary told him the RAF had shot down 183 German planes compared to a loss of forty.

Two days later, on September 17, Hitler postponed Operation Sea Lion indefinitely. The fighting was far from over, but the Royal Air Force had succeeded in defending Britain.

—————◆—————

In the days and months that followed, RAF fighters continued to patrol the skies, watching for German bombers and fighters.

On September 24, 609 Squadron flew to intercept a raid headed for Southampton. The pilots spotted anti-aircraft fire over the Isle of Wight in the English Channel and flew toward the island. Ogilvie saw about a dozen Dornier 17s. He attacked one at about 20,000 feet (6,000 metres) and set its port engine on fire. The Dornier dove straight down. Ogilvie waited for it to crash into the Channel. Much to his surprise and embarrassment, the bomber levelled off and flew away.

Ogilvie raced after it. As he approached the Dornier, it shot oil from a flame-thrower in its tail, but it failed to ignite and coated his windshield instead. The oil prevented Ogilvie from seeing the bomber well enough to fire at it. He almost rammed it, but instead ended up firing at the Dornier until he ran out of ammunition and had to return to Middle Wallop. He suspected the Dornier also returned to its base across the Channel.

Around noon the next day, the squadron flew near Bristol in southwest England. It confronted a large formation of German Dornier and Heinkel bombers, escorted by Messerschmitt fighters. Ogilvie fired at a Dornier and knew that he hit it when glycol, a liquid coolant, streamed from its two engines.

Suddenly, Ogilvie heard a loud noise. A Messerschmitt 109 had fired at him, putting a hole in his starboard (right) wing. He then saw the 109 close behind him; it fired again. Bullets hit various parts of Ogilvie's Spitfire. One went through his tail, one hit his radio, and another hit his port wing.

Despite the damage, Ogilvie flew away from the fighter and pursued the German bombers. He lost sight of the Dornier he had previously attacked, but found another one, which he fired at. Smoke spewed from an engine, but he couldn't shoot it down because he ran out of ammunition and had to return to his base. When he landed, his Spitfire almost turned over because the wheel on his port side no longer functioned properly. The bullet that hit his wing had punctured a tire that retracted into the wing when the Spitfire was airborne.

On September 26, the squadron flew again at 4:00 p.m. It attacked a force of sixty German bombers and a dozen fighters over Christchurch, not far from Bournemouth. Ogilvie confronted a Messerschmitt 109 and fired at it, but it dove away. He then found a Heinkel bomber, got close to its tail and fired. He could see yellow flashes as the bullets hit the bomber. The gunner fired back. Several bullets bounced off the Spitfire's wings. One went through the main spar that supports the wings, but Ogilvie kept flying. He had to end the attack when he was out of ammunition again. Discouraged, he flew back to his base.

The following day, just before noon, the squadron was called upon to attack German bombers and fighters heading for Bristol. Ogilvie flew behind Pilot Officer Mick Miller. A Messerschmitt 110 fired its cannons at Miller. Immediately afterwards, Miller's Spitfire collided with the German fighter. There was a terrific explosion, a sheet of flames arose and then a column of black smoke. Ogilvie saw the wing of the Spitfire flutter to Earth. Miller was dead.

Ogilvie pulled up, saw a Messerschmitt 109, and pushed the button to fire. Another sheet of flames arose, and the 109 descended to the earth.

When they weren't attacking enemy planes, the pilots often spent time improving their skills, but even practise flying could be dangerous, as well as embarrassing. On December 2, Ogilvie was leading some pilots in his squadron when he became so preoccupied watching them that he forgot to watch where he was landing. His Spitfire overshot the runway, slid on the wet grass and went through a hedge. Ogilvie was not hurt, but the plane was almost a writeoff.

Not all of Ogilvie's days were hectic. As 1940 came to an end, he spent time fighting more mundane battles against the cold, wet English winter. By this time, 609 Squadron had moved from Middle Wallop to the RAF base at Warmwell, which was closer to the Channel. Ogilvie's accommodation at his new base didn't help much with keeping him warm: He lived in a tent.

Toward the end of January 1941, Ogilvie realized he had had only one good flying day during the entire, overcast month. He sometimes wondered if he should have joined the French Foreign Legion. Ogilvie and his squadron mates had a clear strategy for defeating the miserable weather: They went to nightclubs. Occasionally, their escapades became what Ogilvie called "riotous." The squadron, however, managed to survive.

In February, the squadron moved to the RAF base at Biggin Hill, on the south side of London. The move pleased Ogilvie. He regarded the base as the number one fighter station in Britain.

———————◆———————

One day in March, the squadron patrolled above the Channel again. Ogilvie flew with Pilot Officer Jan Zurakowski and Pilot Officer Zbigniev Olenski. The controller warned them to watch for enemy fighters. For a while, Ogilvie didn't see anything, but he suddenly heard something; it was Zurakowski. "Ogie! Ogie!" Zurakowski shouted into his radio. Ogilvie reacted quickly. He looked in his mirror and saw the nose of a Messerschmitt 109 behind him. He flew off, but not before the German fighter put three machine gun bullets in his port wing. One punctured the tire contained in the wing. Despite the puncture, Ogilvie landed his Spitfire safely. He felt lucky.

He also felt lucky that evening when Vivien Leigh, the actress who played Scarlett O'Hara in *Gone with the Wind*, attended a party at the Biggin Hill base. He was thrilled to have a chance to dance with her.

During an afternoon in April, the squadron flew over Dungeness in southeast England. Four Messerschmitt 109s flew above Ogilvie and swiftly swooped down. Ogilvie fired at one and it broke away. As he fired at a second, another aircraft dove at him from the sun.

Ogilvie raised the nose of his Spitfire and fired a short burst of bullets. They all missed, which was fortunate because the aircraft was a Spitfire flown by Pilot Officer Sydney Hill, a member of 609 Squadron. Fortunately, after they landed both pilots saw the humour in what had happened.

At about noon on July 4, 1941, Ogilvie and his squadron left Biggin Hill and flew into a blue sky. They were escorting Blenheim bombers on a flight to the Lille area in France. The fighters flew ahead, behind, and on both sides of the bombers. Ogilvie was thrilled to be part of what he regarded as an "imposing spectacle." Far below him he could see the white streaks in the Channel made by the RAF's Air Sea Rescue launches. The bombers and their escorts flew into anti-aircraft fire when they reached Dunkirk in France, and again when they were over St. Omer, which is farther inland.

Off in the distance, Messerschmitt 109s were climbing high. They positioned themselves to attack the bombers on their way home.

The Blenheims reached the target, dropped their bombs, and headed home. German anti-aircraft guns fired at them, but were ineffective. Suddenly, about fifteen Messerschmitt 109s swooped down. Ogilvie turned to attack them. One of the 109s fired at his Spitfire, hitting it. There was a terrific noise. Ogilvie was thrown against the dashboard and blood sprayed all over the cockpit. Ogilvie felt sick. His port aileron came off. He jettisoned his canopy so that he could bail out and turned the oxygen on full to stay awake. He couldn't believe what had happened. No one warned him. He wondered if his radio had stopped working.

Ogilvie decided to fly back to the Channel. He wanted to bail out over it and hope that a rescue boat would save him. His Spitfire, however, no longer flew smoothly. To continue flying, he had to push the control column to the right.

Suddenly everything was quiet; Ogilvie had apparently become unconscious. Through a haze he could see the propeller sticking straight up and smoke spewed from the engine. He had to get out. He let go of the control column and the Spitfire immediately flipped over, flinging him out. Ogilvie groped for his ripcord and pulled it. Then everything went black.

Back in England, a friend of Ogilvie's, Irene Lockwood, was waiting for him. She was a Canadian from Regina who worked with the British Ministry of Information in London. Her job was to censor letters that the men in the services sent to Canada, to make sure that they contained no information that could help the enemy.

Irene, who had met Ogilvie at a nightclub the previous year, had a date with him that night. She had two tickets to the opening of the American Eagle Club, a social club in London for Americans serving with the British armed forces. Laurence Olivier and Vivien Leigh, the famous actors, were expected to attend. Irene treasured the tickets. She had used all her clothing coupons, as well as coupons provided by relatives, to buy a suitable outfit. She was furious when Ogilvie did not meet her.

The next morning, Squadron Leader Michael Robinson phoned her. "I'm sorry to give you the news, but Keith was shot down in flames," he said. No one saw a parachute. Robinson said Ogilvie had little chance of surviving.

Irene remembered her angry reaction when Ogilvie did not appear the previous night. She felt guilty. She wrote a letter to Ogilvie's parents, Charles and Margaret, expressing her sorrow.

Ogilvie's parents received a telegram on July 5 from the British Air Ministry informing them that their son was missing as a result of air operations on July 4, 1941.

Ogilvie's parachute had opened properly, even though the other pilots in 609 Squadron had not seen it. He had landed in a field.

When he regained consciousness, he was surrounded by French citizens. They tried to help him escape, but he couldn't move. He had been hit twice in his left arm, which was broken, and once in his shoulder. He had also lost a lot of blood.

Soon, an ambulance and German soldiers arrived. One of them spoke to Ogilvie and expressed the words he would rather not have heard: "For you, the war is over."

The German soldiers first took Ogilvie to a hospital in Lille, and later to a hospital in Brussels, Belgium. Ogilvie spent seven months lying on a bed with his left arm in a cast that was raised above him. Maggots got into the cast, but the German doctors told him that the maggots would not harm his arm. They were right; the maggots removed dead and infected tissue, and cleaned the wound by consuming bacteria.

When Ogilvie had recovered, he went to a prison camp at Spangenberg, near Kassel, in central Germany. From there he went to Stalag Luft III, a camp run by the Luftwaffe for Allied Air Force officers. It was located at Sagan, 160 kilometres southeast of Berlin. Ogilvie lived in the camp's north compound.

Stalag Luft III was better than most prison camps and certainly better than German concentration camps. Providing they followed the rules, the prisoners at Stalag Luft III could expect to live through the war and then go home.

After he learned that his son was missing, Charles Ogilvie went for long walks beside the Rideau Canal, which was near his home at 43 Patterson

Avenue in Ottawa. He would come back insisting his son was alive.

On August 27, the Air Ministry sent the Ogilvies a telegram that confirmed what Charles Ogilvie believed. The ministry said the Red Cross had informed them that Ogilvie was alive, although a badly wounded prisoner of war. The Ogilvies then wrote to Irene Lockwood in England to convey this information to her.

◆

The prison camp permitted Ogilvie to write letters to family and friends. He corresponded with Irene. She answered his letters, but she never imagined that she would have a permanent relationship with him.

Ogilvie served as the parcel officer for the north compound. With guards watching, he opened both Red Cross parcels and packages that the prisoners received from home. The guards wanted to make sure nothing got into the camp that the prisoners could use for subversive purposes. Ogilvie had the opposite goal. He wanted, for example, to help his fellow prisoners smuggle radio parts into the camp.

Barbed wire and machine guns kept Ogilvie and his fellow prisoners inside the camp, but wire and guns didn't stop the men from dreaming. They wanted to be on the other side of the wire.

In early 1943, Squadron Leader Roger Bushell, a prisoner who had been a lawyer before the war, started planning a mass escape through a tunnel. The prime goal was to disrupt the German war effort by forcing thousands of Germans to hunt for the escaped prisoners. The plan was code-named Operation 200 because the target was to get two hundred men out of the camp. Bushell headed the escape committee and became known as "Big X."

The prisoners started digging three tunnels, named Tom, Dick, and Harry. When the guards discovered Tom, the prisoners used Dick for storage and concentrated on Harry, which started under a stove in room 23 of hut 104. Harry went in a northerly direction toward pine trees, which were supposed to provide cover for the men as they emerged.

Bushell and the escape committee planned every aspect of the escape, from a system to stop the security guards — known to the prisoners as ferrets — from discovering the tunnel to the production of identification papers the men would need once they were free.

Ogilvie helped the escape committee by obtaining identification papers that a guard carried in his wallet. One day, Ogilvie noticed an older guard's wallet was partly out of his back pocket. Ogilvie removed it. He gave the wallet to another prisoner who took it to a hut in which "forgers" produced identification papers. The forgers photographed the guard's papers and gave the wallet back to Ogilvie.

Then, pointing to the wallet, Ogilvie asked the guard if it was his. Indeed it was. Ogilvie said he found it on the floor. The guard was exceedingly grateful. He said if he lost his wallet he would be sent to the eastern front to fight the Russians. From then on, the old guard couldn't do enough to please Ogilvie and his fellow prisoners.

The material that the prisoners used to construct the tunnel came from a variety of sources. Bed boards became the tunnel's walls, and tin cans that had originally contained powdered milk became part of the ventilation system.

An electric wire came from an unexpected source. An electrician working on the roof of the compound's cook house left a coil of wire on the ground. Flying Officer Gordon King from Winnipeg and another prisoner, Flying Officer Ted White from Midland, Ontario, saw it and grabbed it. They hid the coil inside their long winter coats and took it to a hut.

"Man! Could we ever use that!" said Flight Lieutenant Joe Noble, who was gathering supplies. And they did. The wire helped light the tunnel.

Flight Lieutenant Tom Lane from Austin, Manitoba, was one of the prisoners who helped provide security. As a "goon watcher," he signalled to other prisoners if a guard was approaching hut 104. (Lane's own ordeal is described in Chapter 17, "Eagles at War.")

Lane also had more risky assignments. On several occasions he stood in the hallway of hut 104 while a guard drank coffee or smoked a cigarette in one of the rooms of the hut. Lane's job was to assault the guard if he came out of the room when he might see something that would make him suspicious, but he was to make the assault appear accidental. Better that the Germans reprimanded a prisoner for his conduct than that a guard should discover the tunnel. Lane never had to demonstrate his pugilistic ability, but he was ready to confront the guards if necessary.

While the prisoners tunnelled, Irene Lockwood left the Ministry of Information to join the photographic section of the RCAF at the force's headquarters in London. Starting as a leading aircraftwoman and later becoming a sergeant, she performed various tasks in the photo department, including making prints of airmen who received medals or died. The department would then send the photos to the hometown newspapers of the airmen.

One evening, Irene was enjoying a warm bath in her apartment building, the Challoner Mansions, in the Kensington area of London. This was a wartime luxury, which she had paid for by putting money in a water meter. Irene had no intention of leaving that bathtub for any reason.

An air raid siren started wailing. Irene remained in the tub even though she could hear in the distance the throbbing hum made by German bombers. Then she heard bombs explode. The hum became louder, but Irene was not getting out of that tub.

Suddenly, one of her apartment mates, Helen Baker, rushed into the bathroom. "You've got to get out because it's on its way here, and it sounds as though we're right in the pathway," she said as she grabbed Irene's hair and pulled her out of the tub. The two women crawled under a grand piano.

A bomb struck the neighbourhood about a block away. The explosion shattered every window in the apartment unit. Broken glass fell into the bathtub.

While the two women were still under the piano, an air raid warden opened the door of the apartment and shone a flashlight. "Everything all right in here?" he asked.

Yes, everything was all right. Helen had made sure of that.

Finally, in March 1944, the tunnellers had nearly finished Harry. On March 24, two hundred men quietly assembled in hut 104. They entered in small groups so that the guards would not be suspicious.

During the evening the tunnellers chipped away at the soil near the surface. They were shocked when they removed the last bit of earth and looked out. The exit shaft was several metres short of the trees.

Despite the lack of cover for the men leaving the tunnel, the escape went ahead. The prisoners improvised a method that would enable an escaper to leave the exit shaft without a guard seeing him. A man who had just come through the tunnel would hide in the woods then tug a rope to let the prisoner in the shaft know when he could safely come out.

Late in the evening, the prisoners started going down the shaft under room 23, and getting onto trolleys for the 108-metre journey through the tunnel. The men didn't get through as swiftly as expected. Some were not familiar with the tunnel, others could not move quickly because they wore bulky clothes for the cold weather and carried packages of food. Parts of the roof collapsed a few times. The sand had to be removed before more prisoners could go through the tunnel.

Around midnight, Allied air crews inadvertently created a problem for the escapers. An air raid on Berlin prompted the camp to switch off the electricity to ensure a total black out. The lights in the tunnel went out, further delaying the movement of men.

Ogilvie went through the tunnel just before dawn. He was number seventy-six. He climbed up the shaft and then slithered over the snow to the trees where he joined Flight Lieutenant Lawrence Reavell-Carter. They were waiting for ten men to form a group that would skirt the camp before they split into groups of two. Flight Lieutenant Roy Langlois was lying on the ground near the exit, pulling the rope to signal when men could leave the tunnel.

Flight Lieutenant Michael Shand was the next man out. When he was halfway to the woods, a guard patrolling outside the prison fence walked to the tunnel exit and saw someone in the snow.

He fired a shot and started shouting. Reavell-Carter told Ogilvie he thought the guard had seen them, so he stood up. "Kamerade," he shouted, and then, speaking in German, told the guard not to shoot. The guard advised Reavell-Carter to put his hands up and walk toward him.

As Reavell-Carter surrendered, Ogilvie remained still. The guard had not seen him. Ogilvie crawled away. When he had gone about fifty metres he stood up and ran. Shand was running as well. Ogilvie heard rifle shots fired in their direction. He ran faster. The two men separated and went in different directions. They were the last prisoners to flee into the woods.

Ogilvie planned to go to Yugoslavia, where he hoped to join the anti-German partisans. To go around the camp, Ogilvie first ran in a westward direction, then turned south. He ran for several hours. He came across a road and ran along it, going through a small town. Tired, he started walking. A German cyclist rode by him, speaking angrily. He continued pedalling quickly toward the town.

Ogilvie feared the cyclist would inform police of his presence. He went back into the woods and hid in the underbrush. He felt safe there. For the first time since July 4, 1941, he was on his own. He was free.

———————◆———————

When the men in hut 104 heard the rifle shot they suspected that a guard had discovered the tunnel. Someone in the tunnel shouted words that confirmed their suspicion: "It's finished. It's over."

Flight Lieutenant King, one of the prisoners who took the electrical wire, had been waiting to go down the tunnel. King realized that he was not going to have a chance to escape.

The men in hut 104 responded quickly. They ate the food they were going to carry, and they tried to destroy all the documents and equipment they had assembled, such as compasses. They did not want the guards to confiscate these items.

The guards entered hut 104 and ordered all the men to go outside onto the snow-covered campground. The guards carried machine guns. King feared they were going to shoot him and his fellow prisoners.

The men were forced to strip and were searched. Then, with photos kept on file, guards checked the identity of every resident of the compound to see who was missing. After standing for several hours, the prisoners went back to their huts.

———————◆———————

Guided by a compass, Ogilvie set off again in the evening. He walked through snow, slush, and swamps. He stumbled into trees. By morning he was cold, wet, and exhausted. He came across a farm, but after hearing dogs bark he quickly returned to the woods.

By noon, Ogilvie came to a major highway. When he saw it, he realized he had not gone as far as he would have liked. He remembered the escape committee telling him he should reach the highway on his first night. He crossed the highway and re-entered the woods, where he hid in the underbrush.

Ogilvie started walking again in the evening. Snow fell, which made his trek more difficult. After a few hours, he came to a road. In order to travel more quickly, he walked along it. Half an hour later, two members of the German Home Guard saw him as he crossed a bridge near the town of Halbau. The guards took him to a police station on the highway that he had previously crossed. On the way, Ogilvie reached into his pocket, tore up his maps and identification papers, then dropped the pieces.

After an hour, police took him by car to an inn at Halbau. A German in civilian clothes briefly interrogated him. Two hours later, three other officers who had escaped from Stalag Luft III were also brought to the inn and interrogated.

At about 9:00 a.m., two policemen drove the four men to Sagan, but not back to Stalag Luft III. They went to the town's police station where they were stripped, searched, and put in a cell with about twenty other men who had escaped through the tunnel.

In the cell, Ogilvie learned a massive number of Germans had been diverted from their regular duties to recapture the escapers. This included civilians, the home guard, and police departments. Ogilvie and his fellow officers knew they had succeeded in hindering the German war effort.

German troops soon put the men in trucks and drove overnight to a building with stone walls in Gorlitz, near the Czechoslovakian border. It was a Gestapo prison. Ogilvie was put in a cell with two other escapees.

In a few days, the Gestapo took the men to their headquarters for questioning. The interrogator wanted to know how Ogilvie escaped, who had ordered him to escape, where he was going, whether he had any friends in Czechoslovakia, and how the tunnel was constructed.

The interrogation session lasted about an hour, but Ogilvie did not answer the questions. He gave his name, rank, and RAF number: 42872. He also said he was a career officer, and that he had a duty to try to escape. Unlike some of the officers who escaped, Ogilvie was wearing his military uniform, not civilian clothes. This may have given credibility to his comments. After the interrogation, he went back to the prison cell.

On April 4, a corporal and some guards from the Luftwaffe came for Ogilvie and three other escaped prisoners, Flight Lieutenant Paul Royle, Flight Lieutenant Alfred Thompson, and Flight Lieutenant Albert Armstrong. After being with the Gestapo, Ogilvie was pleased to see Luftwaffe guards again. The guards took the four men to a railway station.

The Germans at the station showed curiosity but not animosity when the four prisoners walked into the waiting room; however, the crowd became quiet when Gestapo officers entered the station. The officers wanted the Luftwaffe guards to produce their identification papers. The guards showed the appropriate papers and they, along with the prisoners, boarded a train back to the prison camp. At Stalag Luft III, Ogilvie was put in a solitary confinement cell.

While there, Ogilvie learned that the Gestapo had shot fifty of his fellow escapees, including Squadron Leader Bushell, who had planned the escape. Ogilvie was shocked. He could hardly believe the Germans would execute prisoners.

Only three of the seventy-six — two Norwegians and a Dutchman — succeeded in getting back to England.

———————◆———————

In London on May 23, Anthony Eden, Britain's foreign secretary, told the House of Commons that the government was investigating a news report from Sweden that German guards massacred prisoners of war at Stalag Luft III.

A month later, Eden said the Gestapo had murdered the prisoners. He noted that they had been killed in small groups, not during a mass escape. The foreign secretary pledged that after the war the British government would bring every German involved in the crime to justice.

While Eden promised retribution, the Air Ministry sent a secret message to the prisoners by radio, telling them to stop trying to escape. The ministry wanted the men to remain in their camps until the Allies could liberate them.

The Germans forcefully encouraged the prisoners to stay in their camps. They put up posters that said police and guards would shoot prisoners who escaped.

With the Russians moving toward Germany from the east, the German government became desperate. It wanted to keep the Allied prisoners away from the Russians. On a cold winter night in January 1945, the guards at Stalag Luft III ordered about 10,000 prisoners to leave the camp.

As the parcel officer, Ogilvie handed out Red Cross packages at the entrance to the north compound as the men departed. The prisoners took what they could carry in knapsacks or pull on sleds.

As he walked through the snow on the long march to Bremen in northwest Germany, Ogilvie often felt like giving up. A friend from the camp, Samuel Pepys, infused Ogilvie with the will to take one more step on his blistered feet and then another. In turn, Ogilvie inspired Pepys to continue walking.

The prisoners marched day after day, week after week. For several months the men had only rudimentary accommodation, such as barns.

Spring came. On May 2, 1945, a British armoured unit liberated Ogilvie and the prisoners who were with him. For Keith Ogilvie, the war was over. Six days later, the war was over for everyone in Europe.

In *Their Finest Hour*, Churchill says the figure given to him of 183 German planes shot down on September 15, 1940, was inflated. After the war he learned that the real number was fifty-six, less than a third of the original estimate. Nevertheless, this toll was too high for the Luftwaffe, which concluded that it could not defeat the RAF at that time.

———◆———

When the Allied troops moved into Germany, Irene's position at the RCAF enabled her to see what had occurred in that country during the war. She printed photos taken by RCAF photographers at the Bergen-Belsen concentration camp, in northwest Germany. The photos showed cremation ovens and piles of bodies thrown into pits.

———◆———

After he returned to England, Ogilvie recuperated in a hospital in Gloucester. He wrote to Irene and suggested they get together. When he called her office in London, her supervisor told him she was on vacation beside Lake Windermere, in the Lake District in northwest England. The supervisor also gave him her address.

Ogilvie went to the lake, and found her room. Wearing his full uniform, he knocked on her door. Irene Lockwood was not only stunned that he had found her, but she was delighted to see that he looked so well and had recovered from his ordeals as a prisoner of war.

———◆———

Ogilvie applied to transfer from the RAF to the Royal Canadian Air Force. This time, the RCAF accepted his application, even though he still did not have a university degree. It could hardly deny that he had gained a considerable amount of experience.

Before he left England, Ogilvie filed a report with MI9, the British intelligence service, about his escape from Stalag Luft III. It described how he got out of the tunnel and watched the German guard walk toward the exit shaft. It also described his experience with the Gestapo in the Gorlitz prison.

He sailed for Canada in July 1945, on the ocean liner *Stratheden*. Back in Canada, Ogilvie worked with the RCAF's welcoming committee that met members of the air force returning from England on ships that docked at Montreal, Halifax, and New York.

Irene sailed home to Canada on the *Queen Elizabeth* on February 15, 1946. She had a cold, rough voyage.

Five days later, when the ship docked in New York, she heard her name on the public address system: "Will Irene Lockwood please report to the purser's office."

She feared something was wrong. Perhaps a member of her family was ill or had died. When she got to the purser's office, she was amazed. Keith Ogilvie stood before her. As a member of the welcoming committee, he knew when Irene would return and he arranged to go to New York to welcome her.

Most passengers on the ship were not allowed to go ashore, but Irene left the ship with her special escort. They both enjoyed seeing New York, particularly a show by comedian Danny Kaye. Irene then took a train to Montreal.

Within a few months of returning to Canada, Irene became engaged to Ogilvie. They got married that summer.

Ogilvie, the career officer, remained in the air force and became a squadron leader. He retired in 1963.

As Anthony Eden had promised, the British government sought the Germans who murdered the fifty officers. After the war, the Royal Air Force investigated the deaths and laid charges against Gestapo agents. In his book *The Longest Tunnel*, Alan Burgess sums up the results of the investigation: twenty-one members of the Gestapo were executed, eleven committed suicide, seventeen received long prison terms, and a few were acquitted. Six had been killed in air raids at the end of the war.

In 2000, the British archives released a previously classified document that showed that the decision to execute the fifty escapers was made at the highest level; Adolf Hitler had participated in the decision. He had hoped that executing the prisoners would set an example that would discourage other prisoners from escaping.

In 1963, the mass escape at Stalag Luft III was turned into the movie, *The Great Escape*. Ogilvie enjoyed the film as a Hollywood production, but he thought many scenes did not portray what really happened. No one, for example, escaped on a motorcycle like Captain Hilts, the character portrayed by American actor Steve McQueen.

Although the characters are composites of real prisoners, one scene resembles the incident in which Ogilvie removed a guard's wallet. In the movie, Flight Lieutenant Hendley, played by James Garner, takes a wallet from Werner, a guard. Werner later tells Hendley that he has lost his wallet, and fears he could be sent to the Russian front. Hendley offers to find the wallet but only if Werner gives him a camera.

The stone wall of Victoria Station that the Dornier bomber scraped remains chipped to this day. The chipping is visible about a metre above the ground, at the entrance of what is now a pub called The Iron Duke.

After the war, Ray Holmes, the pilot whose Hurricane struck the Dornier bomber, resumed his career in journalism in Liverpool. He died in 2005.

Ogilvie never claimed to be the only pilot who fired at the Dornier. He thought as many as six other pilots may have attacked it. However, as the

The Ogilvie family

Keith Ogilvie and his wife, Irene, at a reception in London to commemorate the fiftieth anniversary of the Battle of Britain in 1990.

years flew by, Ogilvie's encounter with the German bomber near Buckingham Palace became legendary. One magazine story contained a photo of the palace with the words "Saved by a Canadian" — a claim Ogilvie never made. An article in the *Ottawa Citizen* on May 28, 1998, quotes Tony Little, a friend of Ogilvie's, as saying Ogilvie gave up trying to clarify what he really did.

What is not a legend is that Ogilvie met the current occupant of the palace. Queen Elizabeth talked to him on September 15, 1990, at a ceremony marking the fiftieth anniversary of the Battle of Britain.

———————◆———————

Irene Ogilvie, who will be ninety-one in 2010, lives in a retirement home in Ottawa. She still remembers the photos she printed of the Bergen-Belsen concentration camp. When she hears younger people denying the Holocaust, she feels like telling them that she saw evidence of atrocities.

———————◆———————

The German doctors' opinion that Ogilvie's arm would heal properly turned out to be correct. He had full use of his arm, even when he golfed. Ogilvie's son, Keith Ogilvie Jr., however, thinks that the cold winters at Stalag Luft III and the forced march across Germany may have contributed to the arthritis that his father suffered later in life.

Keith Ogilvie died in 1998. The Ogilvie family spread some of the ashes of the career officer in the rose garden of the chapel at the Biggin Hill airbase in England.

2
PATCHWORK

An intelligence officer told Warrant Officer Frank Cauley and his ten crewmates that he wanted them to find a German submarine in the Atlantic, several hundred kilometres off the west coast of Ireland. At a pre-flight briefing session, the officer told the crew that the sub was U-625. He knew its number because the Allies had broken the Enigma code that the German Navy used to communicate with its submarines. He also knew the general area where U-625 was located.

Cauley listened carefully. The crew had to sink the sub because it was close to an American convoy carrying troops and supplies to Britain. The airmen were excited because this was their first assignment as a crew.

Cauley, twenty-two, was the navigator on Sunderland flying boat EK591, flown by the Royal Canadian Air Force's 422 Squadron. The

Frank Cauley

Frank Cauley in 1944.

squadron was based at the Royal Air Force station at Castle Archdale, beside Lough Erne in Northern Ireland. Sunderlands were big, powerful aircraft with a fuselage that was like the hull of a boat. They were ideal planes to search for submarines because they could remain in the air for the long patrols needed to spot subs, and could land on water.

EK591 took off at 11:00 a.m. on March 10, 1944. The sky was dull and cloudy. However, by the time the plane reached the search area the weather was good and the sun was out. Warrant Officer Frank Morton, who was in the pilot's seat, flew just a few hundred metres above the Atlantic.

After the plane had been airborne for several hours, Sergeant Jimmy Rushton, a gunner who was in the nose of the Sunderland, came on the intercom. "Hey skipper," he said, referring to Morton. He told the pilot and the rest of the crew that he could see a submarine on the surface about ten kilometres away, on the port side of the plane.

Because of the length of time the Sunderland stayed in the air, a second pilot, Flight Lieutenant Sid Butler, was on board. Butler went to the cockpit when he heard about the sub.

"Do you want to go ahead and do it?" Butler asked Morton.

"No, I think maybe you better," Morton replied. Butler had more experience than Morton. He had spent 800 hours in the air conducting similar searches. Morton, in comparison, was on his first trip. Butler moved into the pilot's seat. As Butler flew toward the sub, the crew electronically rolled out four depth charges on rails under the plane's wings.

Cauley sat at the navigator's table behind the cockpit. He was figuring out their position, which he gave to Flight Sergeant Chuck Holland, the wireless operator, to send to their base in Northern Ireland. It was 52.35 north, 20.19 west.

The plane was only fifteen metres above the ocean when it approached the submarine. Cauley, who was watching out of a window, could see more than a German submarine. Sailors were sunning themselves on the hull while others swam in the ocean. A lone sailor holding a machine gun stood in front of the conning tower.

Butler could do nothing to protect the aircraft from the gunner. If he failed to keep the plane flying in the direction it was going, he would prevent the depth charges from dropping close enough to the sub to destroy it.

The sailor with the machine gun sprayed EK591 with bullets. The plane shuddered.

Butler released the depth charges and flew past the submarine. The depth charges exploded, damaging the sub. Spray from the ocean rose thirty metres in the air.

The bullets fired at the plane made holes underneath the galley on the lower front deck. One was large, about fifteen centimetres in diameter. There were also three dozen small holes. Many of the holes were below the waterline, which meant the plane might sink when it tried to land on Lough Erne before the crew could get out.

◆

After the attack, Butler took EK591 to a higher level, out of the range of any guns still active on the submarine. The plane flew above the sub for about an hour. The crew watched the sailors climb into rubber dinghies. The sub then sank. As the plane circled, a member of the crew at the rear of the aircraft took photos of the dinghies.

Holland, the radio operator, sent a message back to the base to say that the crew had completed the attack and that the German sailors were in dinghies. Cauley plotted the course to take the plane back to its base.

A camera on EK591 photographed German sailors in dinghies.

The crew returned to their usual flight duties, but Sergeant Ted Higgins, the flight engineer, had the difficult task of patching up a plane in midflight. His first job was to cover the large hole. He went to the lower deck and patched it with an emergency leak stopper: a piece of metal that covered the hole.

"OK, it's finished — plugged the big one," Higgins told the crew on the intercom, but he also had a question: "What the hell am I going to do about the small holes?" The problem was that he had nothing he could put into them. After ten minutes he came back on the intercom with a strange answer to his own question: "Let's try chewing gum."

All members of the crew had a package of five sticks of Wrigley's Spearmint gum in their ration boxes. Higgins asked his crewmates to get their gum, chew it, and give it to him. He then put it in the small holes. Cauley and the other crew members thought that was an unorthodox method of repairing a plane, but they were happy to try it. They didn't joke about the gum. Their lives might depend on it keeping the plane afloat when they landed at their marine base.

The flight engineer spent half an hour putting the gum in the holes. He used all fifty-five sticks.

By that time, Morton was back in the pilot's seat. He took the plane up to 3,000 feet (900 metres) in order to freeze the gum. Higgins checked the gum. "It held," he told the crew.

Morton continued flying EK591 back to Lough Erne. Holland, the wireless operator, informed the base about the damage to the plane. The base launched its rescue boats so they would be ready to help if needed.

As the plane descended, everyone in the crew was nervous. All the airmen at the base went to the shore to watch the plane come down. EK591 landed smoothly. The gum stayed in the holes and the plane didn't leak.

"Good show!" Morton said to his crew as motorized dinghies approached the plane to take the men ashore.

———◆———

U-625 was commanded by Siegfried Straub. In his book, *Hitler's U-Boat War*, Clay Blair says Straub issued an order to abandon the sub after assessing the damage. He also sent an SOS to the German navy, which diverted two submarines to search for the crew. They found no trace of the men.

———————◆———————

At the Castle Archdale base, the crew of EK591 spent two days celebrating their successful attack and their equally successful flight home.

The RCAF decided to promote both Morton and Cauley from warrant officers to pilot officers.

The chewing gum that the crew gave up was quickly replaced. The Wrigley company heard that its gum saved their aircraft, and it sent twenty-four packs containing five sticks of gum to each member of the crew.

———————◆———————

Cauley went on to spend another 800 hours in the air searching for German submarines, but he never saw another one. He also helped to escort convoys across the English Channel on June 6, 1944, D-Day, the day the Allies landed on the beaches of Normandy. From his position in the air, he could see that the Channel was filled with Allied ships.

———————◆———————

After the war, Frank Cauley went into the wholesale food business. He also became a city councillor in the Ottawa suburb of Gloucester, and a trustee on the Carleton board of education.

Cauley, who will be eighty-nine in 2010, lives in Ottawa and enjoys talking to students about the Second World War. His wartime service was recently honoured by an Ottawa developer, who decided to name a street after him.

Interviewed at his home, he described how he felt during his ordeal with EK591: "Your survival is your number one feeling. The will to survive supersedes every other feeling that you might have. You fight. You fight for life."

The Wrigley company keeps in touch with him, sending him gum when he speaks in public. Asked whether he still chews gum, Cauley replied, "All the time — I never know when I'll have to patch a 747."

Frank Cauley in 2007.

Ian Darling

3
MARIA'S MEMORY

Sergeant Wilf Renner was ready to press the knob on the bomb-release cord of Halifax bomber JD463. Renner, a twenty-two-year-old bomb-aimer, knew he was just minutes away from Frankfurt, a city in central Germany.

Renner's crew, which flew with the Royal Canadian Air Force's 419 Squadron, left their base at Middleton St. George, in northern England, late on the evening of October 4, 1943. The crew's target was Frankfurt's railway yards.

The sky near Frankfurt was filled with Allied bombers. The pilots, however, could not see the other aircraft well. To avoid detection by German night fighters and anti-aircraft crews, the bombers did not have their lights on.

Wilf Renner

Wilf Renner in 1943.

Lying on a board in the nose of his bomber, Renner suddenly noticed another aircraft too close to JD463. "There's a plane below," he shouted over the intercom. Sergeant Arthur Fare, the pilot, immediately pulled JD463 up, avoiding a collision. Fare continued flying to Frankfurt at about 20,000 feet (6,000 metres).

A few minutes went by. The aircraft flew over the city. Renner pressed the knob. "Bombs away," he said. The plane released incendiary, as well as regular, bombs. "Bomb doors closed."

JD463 bounced up as soon as it dropped its heavy load. Fare maintained a steady course for a minute while a camera automatically took photos that would show where the bombs had landed.

He had started to turn the bomber around for the trip home when searchlights caught it. Ground fire hit an engine on the port side. Fare took the plane down as quickly as possible, to get away from the lights. The speed of the descent pinned Renner to the board on which he had been lying. "We're losing control," Fare said on the intercom. "Be prepared to bail out."

Fare managed to stabilize the aircraft for a few minutes. It flew in a more normal manner, except much slower. The crew got ready to bail out — Renner put on his parachute.

A German night fighter approached JD463 and fired, hitting the bomber. Renner was blown out of the aircraft. He didn't know how he got out of the bomber because he was unconscious, but he may have gone through an escape hatch that the crew had opened.

Renner regained consciousness while falling through the air. He pulled the ripcord to open his parachute seconds before he landed. He had descended into a wooded area of Belgium, near the village of Laneffe, about sixty-five kilometres south of Brussels.

Renner had several fractured ribs, as well as cuts to his hands, arms, and head. He had also lost his flying boots. They had come off his feet either when the night fighter hit JD463, or when he was coming down to Earth.

He heard dogs barking, so he knew he wasn't deep in the woods. People who could help might not be far away. Renner wrapped himself in his parachute to try to stay warm during the cool night.

When dawn came he stood up and started walking. He found a path in the woods and decided to follow it. Before long, two woodsmen with saws on their shoulders walked toward him.

The men noticed Renner's uniform. "Royal Air Force comrade," one said, trying to let the young airman know he had landed in friendly territory. The two men were Walloons, French-speaking residents of Belgium.

"Doctor," said one of the men, using a word in English that he knew. He wanted Renner to understand that they realized he needed a doctor to treat his wounds. The men also used the French word "pantoufles," which means slippers. They realized Renner needed something on his feet before he could walk any significant distance.

One of the woodsmen was Camille Van Laethem. "Restez ici avec lui," Van Laethem said to Renner, who had learned some French at St. Jerome's High School in Kitchener, near his home in Preston, Ontario. "Je cherche un docteur." Renner understood that he should stay with the other woodsman while Van Laethem went for a doctor.

The woodsman who remained offered Renner some of his lunch. Renner wasn't hungry, but he did accept the warm milk the woodsman gave him.

Van Laethem returned a few hours later with Dr. Robert Fanuel. He also brought a pair of "pantoufles" and coveralls that Renner could wear over his uniform.

Dr. Fanuel examined Renner, applied some bandages and explained in French that he would come back in the evening with a person who spoke English. Renner's knowledge of French was sufficient to enable him to understand the doctor's plan.

The two woodsmen remained with him as they waited for the doctor to return. As the sun went down on a pleasant fall day, Dr. Fanuel reappeared with a Roman Catholic priest. Speaking in English the priest told Renner, who was also a Roman Catholic, that they wanted to take him to a home in the area. The doctor would treat him there.

Renner got into the doctor's car and went to a two-storey house in the centre of Laneffe. It was the home of another priest, Father Léon Laboulle. Renner didn't have to ask the priest for a rosary. His mother, Louise Renner, had given him a set of rosary beads that he carried on all his flights, including the flight that brought him to Belgium.

Renner felt blessed. He had escaped from the aircraft, had landed safely, and had met people who were trying to help him, even if he could not communicate well with them. He was, in fact, more blessed than he realized because the priest supported the Belgian Resistance that was fighting the Germans.

Father Laboulle was already looking after two Russians who had been German prisoners working at a coal mine at Charleroi, a city near Laneffe. They had escaped from the mine. The Russians had a room downstairs. Renner had a room upstairs.

Dr. Fanuel came to see Renner several times a week. He recovered well.

Father Laboulle was intrigued to have a Canadian with him. He invited some of his friends to meet Renner because they had not previously met a Canadian.

Lying in bed one day after he had been at the priest's home for about two weeks, Renner was startled when he looked up to see a man in a police uniform. He thought the Gestapo had found him. He was mistaken. The man was not a Gestapo agent but a colonel in the Brussels police force.

A friend of the Resistance, the colonel spoke English and assured Renner he could trust Father Laboulle. He also presented Renner with a few cigars.

While at Father Laboulle's home, a member of the Resistance took Renner's photo to create false identification papers for him. The papers said he was Willy Leon Ravel, who was "un cordonnier" — a shoemaker. Having arrived in Belgium without his shoes, Renner appreciated the irony of his occupation. The priest also arranged for Renner to obtain civilian clothes to replace his air force uniform.

One day, Father Laboulle decided to take his Canadian guest on a motorcycle to a store in downtown Charleroi, to buy him a pair of shoes. On the way, the priest stopped his motorcycle and fired a pistol. He wanted to make sure it worked. Although startled, Renner realized he was riding with a brave, bold priest.

When they arrived in Charleroi, the two men walked up a staircase at the back of a shoe store. The stairs led to an apartment occupied by the owner of the store. They couldn't risk entering the store itself in case someone who didn't support the Allies saw them.

The owner came up the interior staircase. Before he could find a pair of shoes for Renner, he noticed some unwanted customers in his store. "Les Boches," he whispered, using a pejorative word to describe Germans.

Renner looked down the staircase into the store. He could see several men in uniforms. He was not mistaken this time. German soldiers were right below him.

Renner quietly backed away from the staircase in the shoe store. The Germans had not seen him. He didn't know why they were in the store. They might have been looking for him and other Allied airmen, or they might simply have been looking for shoes.

Regardless of what they wanted, they made him nervous. Renner remembered that Father Laboulle had a pistol and wondered if he would have to use it.

The soldiers only stayed in the store for about five minutes, then they left.

The store owner took Renner's shoe size, went down to his store and returned with a set of shoes that fit him. Having helped the Allied airman, the owner offered Renner and Father Laboulle a drink. The two men enjoyed a glass of wine before going back to the priest's home.

◆

Back in Preston, Renner's parents, John and Louise, received a telegram a few days after JD463 failed to return to Middleton St. George. It said their son was missing in action. Six months later they were informed that he was presumed dead. Despite this devastating news, Louise Renner presumed he was alive, a presumption based on her faith.

Renner's parents were not the only people deeply affected by the information about their son, who was an apprentice machinist before the war. It was also dreadful news for Renner's fiancée, Elizabeth Pulbrook. He had become engaged to her before he left Canada.

◆

In early November, a few days after Renner acquired his shoes, Dr. Fanuel came to Father Laboulle's home to convey an urgent message. The doctor had come with a member of a Franciscan order, Brother Materne, to tell Renner and the two Russians that they should leave immediately. The Gestapo were searching the area.

Wilf Renner

Maria Dardenne.

They all left the house within minutes. Renner departed on Brother Materne's bicycle. The ride was not very comfortable because Brother Materne was also on the bike. The priest pedalled while Renner sat on the seat. Renner did not know where he was going. He just had his rosary beads and his faith that this stranger would take him to an appropriate location.

Brother Materne took Renner a few kilometres away from Laneffe, to the home of Dr. Fanuel's aunt.

The doctor had made the right decision when he urged Renner to get out of the house. Within hours, the Gestapo came to Father Laboulle's home and took the priest away for questioning. They held him for a week before releasing him.

Dr. Fanuel's decision to put Renner in his aunt's home was not so wise. She was too nervous to look after an Allied airman. The doctor decided that Renner should go to another home. After he stayed with the aunt for two nights, he again sat on the seat of a bicycle while Brother Materne pedalled.

◆

Renner went about fifteen kilometres, to the home of Maria Dardenne in the hamlet of Fairoul. Maria, who was forty, had a particular reason to support the Belgian Resistance. She hated Germans because her older brother, Raymond, was critically wounded by German soldiers who invaded Belgium during the First World War. Gangrene had developed in his legs and Maria, who was a teenager at the time, took care of him until he died.

Even though twenty-five years had passed since the end of the First World War, she still had a vivid memory of her brother and the way he died. "Les Boches," she said contemptuously when talking about the country that her brother fought.

This memory motivated Maria to look after Allied flyers during the Second World War, when German troops again invaded her country. Renner was not the first flyer she sheltered. She had previously taken in Flight Sergeant Douglas Knight of the Royal Air Force. The Germans eventually caught Knight, who became a prisoner of war. They shot the member of the Resistance who was escorting him at the time.

The Belgian Resistance had offered Maria money to compensate her for looking after the Allied evaders who stayed with her, but she wouldn't accept any compensation. She didn't want to be paid for helping flyers who risked their lives to fight Nazi Germany.

Maria lived in a large stone house that had two storeys and an attic. Renner stayed in a room on the second floor. Maria's eighty-four-year-old father, Joseph Dardenne, lived in another room on the same floor. She did not tell her father about Renner because she thought they would all be safer if few people knew about him.

Maria's father stayed in his room most of the time, coming out to go across the street with her to eat meals at the farm operated by her brother, Joseph Dardenne Jr.

Joseph Jr. knew Renner was hiding in Maria's house, and he also knew what happened to the person who was escorting the previous Allied evader Maria had sheltered. "Prenez garde. Prenez garde," he said to his sister as he urged her to be careful. He was concerned not only for his sister, but also for himself, his father, his wife, and his infant son, who was born the week Renner arrived.

Most of the time, Renner remained in his room. He would go out to use the washroom, and when the father left the house. Even in his room he had to be careful. The room faced the street and he did not want anyone in the hamlet to see him through the window.

If Renner did have to hide quickly, he could go to another bedroom that had a trap door to the attic. For added security, Maria and Joseph Jr. had strung an electrical wire between their homes. Anyone in the farmhouse could use the line to activate a buzzer in Maria's kitchen if a suspicious person approached.

Maria was concerned about security even when she did the laundry. After she washed Renner's clothes, she would hang them inside hers on a clothesline so neighbours would not see them. She also used her coat to cover the food she brought from the farmhouse to his room every evening after she finished working on her brother's farm.

During his first few months at Maria's home, Renner studied French. Maria helped him, and gave him a dictionary and newspapers. The French he learned at St. Jerome's High School quickly came back to him.

He also helped Maria to learn English. She found the language to be exasperating and asked him to explain why certain grammar rules existed. Renner, not an English scholar, did his best.

Renner spent a lot of time on his own. Elisabeth Neuville, the sister of a local Resistance leader, brought him two English books. The first was the complete works of William Shakespeare; the second was a copy of Reader's Digest from 1926. His favourite Shakespearean play was *Hamlet*. Renner's confinement enabled him to understand Hamlet's isolation and introspection.

To get some fresh air, Renner would go to the courtyard at the back of the house, but he could do that only when no one was around.

He and Maria occasionally left the house after dark. Sometimes they went to her brother's house, where Joseph Jr. told Renner about the progress of the war. They also went to see two other Allied airmen in Fairoul who were evading the Germans, Sergeant Charles Warren, an American, and Sergeant Alan Lucas, an Englishman. They stayed with the village priest.

In February 1944, another evader arrived at Maria's home and stayed in a room on the second floor. He was Sergeant Norm Michie, a Canadian from Toronto who had been shot down over the Netherlands.

With two evaders on the second floor, Maria's father realized strangers were in his home. Maria told him they were members of the

Belgian Resistance who were staying overnight. Even though the father had seen them, Renner and Michie tried to stay away from him.

Some days the house was even more crowded. Brother Materne stayed there if he was travelling on behalf of the Resistance and needed a place to sleep.

Despite the stress of working with the Resistance, or perhaps because of it, Maria maintained a sense of humour. Once, when Désiré Croin, the head of the local movement, visited her house she offered him a cigarette she had rolled. It contained not only tobacco, but also the end of a match. Croin, who had a moustache, smoked the cigarette contentedly until the match flared and singed his moustache.

Renner and Michie talked to members of the Resistance when they came to Maria's house. In particular, they could easily talk to Elisabeth Neuville. She spoke English well because she had studied in England before the war. Her brother, Walter Neuville, was the second in command of the local movement.

These conversations prompted the two evaders to think of joining the Resistance. They felt restless, and they wanted to help the war effort. They also thought the Resistance might eventually help them get back to England.

———◆———

By mid-April, the winter had receded, and the Resistance in the area, known as Secret Army Zone 1C60, could concentrate on putting men in the woods. Croin, the head of the zone, and Neuville accepted the offer of the two airmen to join their Resistance group.

For Renner and Michie, leaving Maria was emotionally difficult. She had risked her life for them.

The two men walked for several hours to a camp that the Resistance had set up in a wooded area near the town of Walcourt. On his first night in the camp, Renner felt apprehensive. He had left the relative security of Maria's house and he did not know what would happen next.

The camp was composed of two huts. One became the home of seven men: Charles Warren and Alan Lucas, who were the two other evaders in Laneffe; Pat Healey, a Canadian evader from Montreal; two Russians; and Renner and Michie. Two Yugoslavians lived in the other hut.

Renner's hut provided rudimentary accommodation. About five metres by five metres, it was made of tree branches, parachute silk, and straw.

The men at the camp had a specific job to perform. They were responsible for retrieving supplies that the Royal Air Force occasionally dropped by parachute.

The group was always prepared, in case the Germans raided the camp. They wore their clothes at all times. They were also armed with Sten submachine guns. The Russians and Yugoslavians carried the guns. Those men were particularly tough.

A member of the Resistance came to the camp each day. In addition to bringing items needed for daily living, the visitors would tell the men when to expect an aircraft. The Resistance received information about the flights through shortwave broadcasts on the British Broadcasting Corp. Neuville had the radio to receive these messages.

The code was the French phrase "la carpe est muette," which means "the carp is silent." Those words designated a particular field near the camp as the drop zone.

The BBC broadcast the code on May 10, 1944. Renner was excited. This was what he had been waiting for. He and his colleagues went to the field in the evening and waited for the plane. The group had four big spotlights. When they heard the engines of a plane, the men shone the lights on the area where they wanted the pilot to drop the supplies.

Each drop included about ten or twelve canisters, and weighed about nine tons. The canisters, containing items such as guns, ammunition, and cigarettes, came down without any complications. The men went to them, removed the parachutes, sorted the contents, and hid the supplies in the woods for the night. The next day a member of the Resistance came to the camp in a truck to collect them.

The supplies were well protected. Belgian police, quietly working with the Resistance, travelled with the load, just in case problems arose on the way.

The Royal Air Force dropped supplies near the camp on two other nights during the spring and summer. Because the men in the camp could go several weeks without having to retrieve canisters and sort the supplies, they had a lot of free time. During this time the English-speaking men talked with the Russians and the Yugoslavians in broken French, which was their only common language. They spoke about their home countries, their families, and the war.

The three Canadians — Renner, Michie, and Healey — commiserated with each other. Even though winter was over, the camp was cold, and they wondered when they would get back to Canada.

One day the men in the camp collected some money they had accumulated and asked a member of the local Resistance to buy a few bottles of gin. That night, the camp had a party atmosphere.

On June 6, the camp had a different kind of celebration. On this day, Neuville and his sister came to say that the Allies had landed on the Normandy beaches. It was D-Day, the day the men in the camp had been waiting for. From then on, they wondered when Allied troops would arrive in Belgium.

———————◆———————

A Belgian army officer came to the camp with a member of the Resistance in early September, to tell them that the American Third Army had liberated the area. For Wilf Renner, the war was over.

Renner and Michie went back to Fairoul, and stayed with Maria for a few days. They quickly saw how the Germans had lost their power. Brother Materne brought a seventeen-year-old German soldier he had captured to the house. He put the soldier on a bed and chained him to a metal railing. The next day he took the prisoner away.

Maria finally introduced Renner and Michie to her father, the person they had tried to avoid meeting.

While at Maria's home, Renner and Michie received British uniforms and were taken to an American base at Brussels. At the base, the Americans interrogated Renner to determine if he really was an Allied evader and not a German spy. He then flew to London, where the British interrogated him again. Finally, he was released to the RCAF.

The air force informed Renner's parents that their son was alive and well. Even though Louise Renner had not heard anything about her son for almost a year, she always believed he was alive.

Renner came home on the *Queen Mary*, which docked in New York. He arrived back in Preston on October 31, 1944. Less than a month later, on November 25, he married Elizabeth.

He remained in the RCAF and stayed at several bases. He was prepared to participate in the war against Japan, but the air force discharged him in May 1945, the month the war against Germany ended.

JD463 crashed near the village of Thy-le-Château. All of Renner's crewmates died. The bodies of three were found in the wreckage of the plane. The other three, blown out of the aircraft, were found on the ground.

The members of the crew are buried in the Gosselies Communal Cemetery, near Charleroi: Sergeant Arthur Fare, the pilot; Sergeant Cyril Winterbottom, the flight engineer; Sergeant George Chapman, the navigator; Sergeant William Boyce, the wireless operator; Sergeant George Beach, the mid-upper gunner; and Sergeant Robert Paddison, the rear gunner.

Paddison was from the Collingwood area in Ontario. He, like Renner, was a member of the RCAF. The other members of the crew served with the RAF.

In their book, *The Bomber Command War Diaries*, Martin Middlebrook and Chris Everitt say 406 aircraft participated in the raid on Frankfurt. The raid caused severe damage to the eastern part of the city and the docks on the River Main. The two writers also say a bomb landed on an orphanage, killing ninety children, fourteen nuns, and other staff members.

After the war, Renner resumed his pre-war career as a machinist. With two partners he set up Galt Wood Tool and Machine Co., in 1956. He sold the company in 1976, stayed on as an adviser, and fully retired in 1986. He served his community by accepting several board positions, including chair of the Waterloo County Catholic School Board.

In 1961, Renner returned to Belgium to see Maria in peace time. He saw her three other times. She died in 1977 at the age of seventy-four.

Renner wanted to do something in Fairoul to honour Maria. After consulting her family, he donated a new altar to the village church in her memory.

On a trip to Belgium in 1992, he went to the woods where he had camped with the Resistance. "Thank goodness it's only once in a lifetime," he said to himself as he looked around. He also visited the graves of his crewmates.

The pilot of the night fighter that shot JD463 down was Major Wilhelm Herget. He was the commander of Nachtjagdgeschwader 4, a group of Luftwaffe night fighters based at Florennes, Belgium.

Herget went to Belgium after the war to identify himself as the pilot who shot down the bomber at Thy-le-Château. He spoke to a historian, Jean Léotard. He also said that at the end of the war an American tank shot his plane down and he became a prisoner of war.

Wilf Renner still lives in Preston, which is now part of the City of Cambridge, and he still has the rosary he carried with him throughout the war. He will be ninety in 2010.

Renner's respect for Maria Dardenne remains as strong today as ever. He has a large picture of her in the living room of his home. Renner requires only a few words to describe the woman who protected him: "Maria was the bravest woman I ever met."

Wilf Renner in 2008.

Ian Darling

4
A FLIGHT FOR MALTA

Flight Sergeant Bob Middlemiss had never taken off from an aircraft carrier before. He was apprehensive.

Middlemiss, a member of the Royal Canadian Air Force who was flying with Britain's Royal Air Force, usually took off from airfields, but he was eager to help the RAF get Spitfires to Malta, which is in the middle of the Mediterranean Sea.

Spitfires could not stay in the air long enough to fly directly from England to Malta, which was a British colony during the war. To get the planes to Malta, the RAF decided to disassemble them and put the parts on a freighter sailing from Greenock, Scotland, to Gibraltar, at the western end of the Mediterranean. At Gibraltar, mechanics reassembled the planes and put them on HMS *Eagle*, an aircraft carrier.

Bob Middlemiss

Bob Middlemiss in 1941.

Closely guarded by several destroyers, the *Eagle* and its cargo of thirty-one Spitfires sailed toward Malta.

On June 3, 1942, the *Eagle* reached a point north of Algiers, from which Middlemiss and the other pilots could fly to Malta in about three hours.

Middlemiss, who was twenty-one, revved his Spitfire's engine. He pushed the throttle forward to have maximum power. Then the ground crew pulled the wood chocks from in front of the wheels and the Spitfire rolled along the short deck then dipped down when it left the carrier. Middlemiss was just a few metres above the sea, but he pulled up into a bright, sunny sky.

Three other Spitfires flew close by. When the four planes were close to Malta, several Messerschmitt 109s appeared suddenly and started firing. Because a Spitfire could turn quickly, Middlemiss escaped from the German fighters.

One of his colleagues was not so fortunate. The 109s shot him down. The Germans also shot down three other Spitfires flying to Malta that day. Of the thirty-one Spitfires that left the *Eagle* that day, only twenty-seven landed on the island.

When Middlemiss arrived at the Takali airbase in the middle of Malta, he realized how desperately the RAF needed the Spitfire he had just flown: Another pilot was already waiting to take off in it.

◆

Malta, the largest island in the Maltese archipelago, was under siege. The entire archipelago is only 316 square kilometres, the size of a metropolitan city. During the Second World War, however, Malta had a strategic importance far greater than its size. Located between Italy and North Africa, Malta was a fortress from which a country with a navy and an air force could stop an opponent from dominating the Mediterranean Sea.

The Allies used Malta to attack ships taking supplies to German troops in North Africa that were advancing toward British positions in Egypt. For the Allies, losing Malta would have meant losing the Mediterranean.

Nazi Germany and Fascist Italy fully understood the importance of Malta. Planes from both countries bombed the island relentlessly. They also attacked British ships sailing for the island. As a result, the British navy sometimes used submarines to bring in supplies.

The Allied forces were short of food, fuel, guns, and ammunition. On some occasions, the Royal Air Force had no fighter aircraft ready to fly. The island was short of everything needed to win a war, except for spirit and determination.

Middlemiss's arrival in Malta was part of the RAF's campaign to build up its forces on the island in order to end the siege. A member of the RAF's 249 Squadron, Middlemiss quickly learned how the siege could affect even a strong young man such as himself. He normally weighed about 140 pounds, but the shortage of food cut that figure by ten to fifteen pounds. In addition, Middlemiss suffered from what became known as Malta Dog, which was a form of dysentery.

———◆———

Middlemiss and his squadron were often called on to pursue German aircraft that had left Sicily to attack Malta. On July 7, 1942, just over a month after he arrived on the island, Middlemiss was at his airfield early in the morning, ready for another day of flying. The weather was ideal: the sun shone, the sky was blue.

Later in the morning a radar unit detected enemy aircraft approaching Malta. The controller, who worked in a bombproof shelter in Valletta, Malta's biggest city, called for eight of the squadron's Spitfires to take off. He kept two pilots in reserve: Middlemiss and Flight Lieutenant Raoul Daddo-Langlois.

Middlemiss and Daddo-Langlois did not want to be left behind — they wanted to participate in the attack. Daddo-Langlois told officers at the Takali base that he and Middlemiss wanted to get their Spitfires into the air. The officers relayed the information to the control centre. After several minutes, the controller agreed. He let the two pilots take off.

Middlemiss was already wearing his Mae West life preserver. All he had to do was step on the port wing of his Spitfire and climb into the cockpit. He put on his helmet and mask, and snapped on his parachute and uninflated dinghy. He taxied the Spitfire out of the sandbagged enclosure where it was kept when not in use.

Daddo-Langlois and Middlemiss flew south, in an attempt to gain altitude before confronting the German planes. The two pilots had time to turn northward, but they did not have time to climb to their maximum altitude before they spotted Messerschmitt 109 fighters escorting Junkers Ju 88 bombers. Daddo-Langlois and Middlemiss also didn't have time to position themselves so that the sun was behind them; the German pilots could already see them.

"Shall we have a go?" Daddo-Langlois asked over his radio. Middlemiss said they should attack the German planes. Daddo-Langlois fired at a bomber and hit it. Middlemiss noticed that one of the 109s was close to the tail of Daddo-Langlois' Spitfire. Middlemiss fired machine-gun bullets and cannon shells at the fighter. The 109 exploded.

Middlemiss wanted to get away as quickly as possible because he suspected that the pilot of the fighter he shot down might have been paired with another pilot. He turned his Spitfire left to break away, but he was too late. As Middlemiss leaned forward and looked to his left, the pilot of another 109 fired at his plane. At least one shell hit the starboard side of his Spitfire's fuselage.

Either a shell, or a piece of the aircraft hit by the shell, flew into the cockpit, striking the muscles in Middlemiss's back and right arm. That was the arm he used to adjust the control column, which moved the plane's ailerons.

Although he didn't feel any pain, he knew he had to get out of the aircraft. The Spitfire started spinning to the left. He didn't even have time to send a Mayday message. Middlemiss tried to bail out, but he was pinned inside the plane by the centrifugal forces produced by the spin. Before he could get out he had to stop the spin. To do that, Middlemiss used his left hand to push the control column forward and his right foot to turn the starboard rudder.

He stopped the spin, pulled the small rubber ball above him to jettison the cockpit canopy, rolled the plane over, and fell out.

———————◆———————

Middlemiss managed to pull his ripcord, probably with his left hand. His descent to Earth was quiet and gentle. The thought of going into the Mediterranean Sea did not overly concern him. He felt thankful that his parachute had opened. He would deal with the sea when he had to.

As he came down, Middlemiss remembered from his training that parachutists have trouble judging their distance from the water. He needed to know the distance because he wanted to release his parachute just before he entered the water. If he didn't release the chute, the wind could drag him along the sea and prevent him from inflating his dinghy. To get a better idea of the distance, he dropped one of his flying boots. The boot took some time to reach the surface, so he knew he was not ready to release his parachute.

He descended further, and released his chute as he hit the water. Once he was in the water, Middlemiss inflated his Mae West life jacket with a small bottle of carbon dioxide. It kept him afloat.

He had only one thought: to get into his dinghy. First he had to inflate it — he found the canister of carbon dioxide for that purpose, pulled a pin, and turned the handle slowly. Nothing happened. No carbon dioxide flowed to inflate the dinghy. He turned the lever the other way and, again, nothing happened.

In addition to the canister, Middlemiss had a small hand pump that was attached to the dinghy by a cord. He decided to use it. As he tried to connect the pump to the valve, the cord got in his way. He pulled out a hunting knife from inside his life jacket and cut the cord. The pump was free. Then, with his left hand, he twisted the pump onto the valve. Gradually, he was able to inflate the dinghy and climbed in.

When he was in the dinghy, Middlemiss felt relief. The sea was calm, so his chances of surviving for a while were reasonably good, but he did wonder whether sharks would find him before his squadron did. Just in case any sharks did approach, he had a packet of shark repellent in his rescue kit.

Middlemiss's squadron sent several Spitfires to look for him. However, the pilots searched the wrong part of the Mediterranean. The squadron thought he was northwest of Malta, but he was northeast of the island.

After Middlemiss had been in the dingy for a few hours, two Spitfires flew over him. They had been protecting minesweepers in the area. Although Middlemiss could not tell from the dinghy who was in the planes, the pilots were Sergeant Paul Brennan and Sergeant Louis de l'Ara. Both were members of his squadron.

At first, Middlemiss was concerned, in case the pilots did not know he was an Allied flyer. He had no means of communicating with them. The planes passed over him a second time. This time they waggled their wings, a sign that they had spotted him and would report his location to the RAF's Air Sea Rescue unit in Valletta.

"Thank Heavens," Middlemiss said to himself. He assumed the pilots had seen his bright yellow Mae West life jacket, an item worn only by Allied flyers. He now had reason to hope he would be rescued.

A short time later, the RAF's Air Sea Rescue launch No. 128, under the command of Flight Sergeant Harrison, came for him. The crew threw a climbing net over the side of the boat and helped Middlemiss come aboard. They wrapped him in blankets and put him in a chair. A member of the crew gave him a drink of rum. "Get this down," he said. The launch then headed for Valletta.

An ambulance took Middlemiss from the rescue launch to a military hospital at Mtarfa, which was near the Takali base. Captain Rankin, a doctor at the hospital, later told Middlemiss he was fortunate to have leaned forward when the 109 attacked him. That may have saved his life

— the shell or debris that struck him would have gone through his lungs if he had been sitting back.

While Middlemiss recovered, the air war continued. From a balcony in the hospital he could see German planes attacking the airbase. Within a few weeks, Middlemiss was well enough to return to England, where he served as an instructor. He went on to have a full tour with 403 Squadron, during which he flew Spitfires over France and the Netherlands. He also flew a few flights with 442 Squadron.

HMS *Eagle*, the aircraft carrier that brought Middlemiss toward Malta, was torpedoed and sunk by a German submarine shortly after Middlemiss left the island. It was one of four aircraft carriers escorting a convoy taking supplies to Malta.

The siege of Malta came to an end in late 1942. The Allies had shown that they would not give up the island. In his book on the air war over Malta entitled *Hell Island*, Dan McCaffery wrote, "On paper they (the Allied forces on Malta) could not possibly win. But they did. And in the process they altered the outcome of the entire war."

Raoul Daddo-Langlois, the pilot with whom Middlemiss flew when he was shot down, was killed in 1943, while flying over Sicily.

Middlemiss returned to Canada, on the ocean liner *Aquitania*, in the spring of 1944. He foresaw a postwar conflict with the Soviet Union and decided to stay in the air force. He remained in the service until he retired in 1969, rising to the rank of wing commander.

Now living in Barrie, Ontario, Middlemiss is the honorary colonel of 427 Squadron, a special operations aviation squadron at Canadian Forces Base Petawawa. He will be ninety in 2010.

Bob Middlemiss's time in Malta was relatively short, but it was long enough for him to have the satisfaction of knowing that he participated in one of the most crucial air battles of the Second World War.

Bob Middlemiss takes the salute during a Battle of Britain commemorative ceremony in Barrie, Ontario, in 1999.

5
FINAL DESCENT

As Flight Sergeant Harry Denison settled into the mid-upper turret of Halifax bomber NP799 he was told that the plane that had taken off ahead of him had crashed, having gone only about a kilometre. The crash may have been caused by ice forming on its wings.

It was March 5, 1945, and the airbase at Linton-on-Ouse in Yorkshire, England, was cold and misty. Denison and his crew were tired. They had been on a long flight to Germany the night before.

Despite the weather, Denison's pilot, Flight Lieutenant Jack Kirkpatrick, rolled NP799 down the tarmac runway after the crew had checked their equipment. Denison, a farm boy who grew up near Vernon in the interior of British Columbia, checked, as he always did, to make sure his parachute was clipped to the plane's fuselage near his turret.

Harry Denison

Harry Denison in 1943.

Kirkpatrick, Denison, and the rest of the crew were members of the Royal Canadian Air Force's 426 Squadron. All of the crew were Canadians, except for Sergeant Ian Giles, who was from Dumbarton, Scotland, and a member of Britain's Royal Air Force. He had been surprised when he was asked to join a Canadian crew, but mixing the composition of flight crews was common during the war.

That night they were flying to Chemnitz, a city in eastern Germany. At a pre-flight briefing, the crew was told that Chemnitz was the site of factories making items, such as ball bearings, for the German military.

As NP799 left England, the weather improved. Denison looked out of the dome above his turret in the middle of the plane. He was watching for German night fighters that could approach swiftly and fire on the heavy, slow-moving bomber.

To avoid detection, NP799 and the other bombers maintained radio silence. They also kept their lights off.

Kirkpatrick was flying NP799 on a steady course at about 14,000 feet (4,200 metres). When the bomber was about an hour away from Chemnitz, the pilot started to climb to 22,000 feet (6,600 metres). He wanted to prevent the bomber from becoming easy prey for the anti-aircraft guns protecting the city.

Denison kept watching. Neither he nor anyone else in his crew saw anything unusual. It had been an uneventful flight, but suddenly Denison heard an explosion. Something had hit the plane.

The dome of the gun turret shattered. A piece of the heavy plastic in the dome fell on Denison's head, cutting him from his right ear to his chin.

Bleeding profusely, Denison slipped out of his turret seat and dropped to the floor. He wanted to get his parachute and attach it to his harness.

Unable to see in the dark, Denison didn't know what had caused the explosion. He didn't know if a night fighter had fired on the bomber, or if another bomber had accidentally collided with NP799. He also didn't know that NP799 was completely breaking up. He was rapidly descending in just the centre section of the bomber's fuselage — half the body of the plane.

———◆———

Denison was completely immobile. As the bomber hurtled toward Earth, the inertial forces pinned him to the fuselage floor so that he couldn't reach his parachute. He thought about his crew: Kirkpatrick, the pilot; Giles, the flight engineer; Flying Officer Bob Fennell, the navigator; Flying Officer Bud Stillinger, the bomb-aimer; Pilot Officer Jack Larson, the wireless operator; and Pilot Officer Roald Gunderson, the tailgunner. Were they still alive? Denison couldn't see or hear any of them.

Then he thought of his family: his father, Norman, and mother, Ethyl, back on their farm in British Columbia. How would they feel when they learned that their son had been killed?

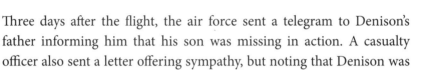

Three days after the flight, the air force sent a telegram to Denison's father informing him that his son was missing in action. A casualty officer also sent a letter offering sympathy, but noting that Denison was not necessarily dead. His mother never gave up hope that her son was alive; his father was less sure.

As the bomber came down the wind shrieked around the fuselage like a hurricane. Unable to do anything to save himself, he was certain that he was going to die as soon as the plane crashed on the ground.

After the fuselage came crashing down, Denison lay unconscious on the floor near the turret for seven or eight hours. Snow swirled around him. When the sun came up, Denison slowly regained consciousness. His entire body was bruised. He vomited heavily. He didn't remember hitting the ground, presumably because he was unconscious at that point.

He tried to check the time, but his watch broke into pieces when he moved his arm. The watch had been crushed during his descent. He also noticed that a metal key he kept in a pocket had broken into two pieces.

Denison crawled outside. He was in a replanted pine forest, west of Chemnitz. He could see the trees that the fuselage may have struck, reducing the speed at which it hit the snow-covered ground.

He looked for his crewmates, but he couldn't see them. In fact, he couldn't see much of NP779. He could see only the section of the fuselage in which he had been trapped, which was only about six metres long. The nose, cockpit, tail, and the two wings had become separated from the fuselage some time after the explosion.

Later that morning, Denison wandered along a trail and found a stream. He wanted to drink from it. He was so weak, however, that he collapsed into the water and had to pull himself out. He then removed his parachute harness to make moving easier.

He thought he was alone, but then he heard noises. He screamed for help. Some men wearing grey pyjama-like uniforms approached. They were slave labourers who were cutting wood. They carried him to their base, which was a German army camp. The commanding officer spoke some English and wanted to know where Denison had put his parachute. He tried to explain that he had come down without one.

The officer took him by car to a nearby hospital where German doctors treated his head wound and a broken rib. He spent about a month recuperating in a ward with other prisoners of war.

When the hospital released Denison, a short guard with a rifle escorted him on a train to an interrogation camp at Frankfurt. After a few days, he and some other prisoners were taken, again by train, to Dulag Luft III, a prisoner of war camp near Wetzlar.

◆

In early April, after Denison had been at Dulag Luft III about a week, the German troops at the camp told the prisoners to pack their belongings and get ready to move. They were going on a forced march. The Allies were pressing on all fronts, and Germany's leaders were getting worried. German authorities wanted to move the prisoners away from the Allies. The Germans told the prisoners to start marching southward.

Despite being released from hospital, Denison was still not in the best of health. He was limping and the cut on his face had not completely healed. Still wearing the same uniform he was wearing the night of his last flight, Denison started walking through the German countryside in wet, miserable weather.

Some of the prisoners were exhausted. Others were so sick with illnesses, such as dysentery, that they stopped walking. German guards used their rifle butts to encourage the prisoners to keep marching.

Denison made up his mind that he was not going to give up. Somehow, he was going to survive. Somehow, he was going to return home. Denison and his fellow prisoners were taken to a railway siding and herded onto open rail cars — the kind that might have been used to carry gravel.

All of a sudden, the prisoners heard planes coming toward them. There were a total of seventeen aircraft, and they were flying fast and low.

Denison ran from the train as quickly as he could. His life was in danger again, but not from German troops. The planes were American fighters: sixteen Thunderbolts and one Lightning. The pilots didn't know they were about to fire on a train carrying prisoners of war.

Denison got about a hundred metres away and started looking for any kind of shelter. He fell into a ditch. The planes dropped bombs on the train and then, moments later, came back firing cannon shells. Denison felt something warm hit his head. It was an empty shell case.

German troops on two flatbed rail cars fired anti-aircraft guns at the planes, but the fighters destroyed the train, killing the gun crews. Denison survived the attack without being injured. From then on, however, he and the other prisoners refused to go on a train. They insisted they travel only on roads. The German guards agreed. By that time, they weren't keen to travel by train either.

The prisoners scrounged food, such as potatoes and sugar beets, and they slept wherever they could. One evening, Denison slept in a barn next to a family of pigs. After marching for seventeen days, the prisoners arrived at Stalag VIIA, which was near Munich.

While at the camp, Denison sent a postcard to his parents, informing them that he was well, considering what he had experienced. He told them he had fully recovered from his injuries, except that his back still ached. He made only one request: "Please don't worry about me."

On Saturday, May 5, the prisoners went to sleep not knowing that a significant change was about to occur. When they woke up, the German guards were gone. They had fled in advance of the arrival of American troops in General George Patton's Third Army. For Harry Denison, the war was over.

The prisoners remained at Stalag VIIA until the Americans could take them to a nearby airstrip, from which they flew to Rheims, France.

Denison was there on May 8, which became VE Day — Victory in Europe Day. He didn't do much celebrating, however. The prisoners were getting rid of the lice they had attracted. His clothes were washed, but he continued to wear the same uniform he had worn since March 5. Three days later, he boarded a Lancaster bomber that was being used as a transport plane. Peering out of a window, Denison saw the best sight he had ever seen: the shores of England.

Weighing only 119 pounds instead of his usual 170, Denison was taken to a hospital in Bournemouth after he landed, where he stayed for about a month. He finally received fresh clothes.

While at Bournemouth, he sent a telegram to his parents to tell them he was alive and well. Until then, Norman and Ethyl Denison knew only that their son was missing. The postcard Denison sent from the prison camp had not arrived.

———◆———

Denison returned to Canada on the ocean liner *Ile de France*. When he arrived at Halifax, he boarded a train filled with servicemen who had been prisoners of war. Although the former prisoners were returning home, the trip was not as exhilarating as Denison had expected. It was stressful. The air force had released information that enabled the relatives of his crewmates to meet him as the train came to stations near them. When the train pulled into Montreal, the family of Jack Larson, the wireless operator, approached him and wanted to know what happened to Larson. All Denison could say was, "I don't know." Then the train stopped at Toronto, where the family of Bob Fennell, the navigator, met him. Again, all he could say was, "I don't know." In Winnipeg, the family of Bud Stillinger, the bomb-aimer, met him. "I don't know." In Saskatoon, the family of Roald Gunderson, the tailgunner, met him. "I don't know." In Edmonton, the family of Jack Kirkpatrick, the pilot, met him. "I don't know."

Denison got off the main train at Sicamous, B.C., and boarded another train for Vernon, where his family met him. He arrived home several weeks before the postcard he had sent from the German prison camp.

Denison's mother, Ethyl, was so relieved to see her son that she insisted he go with her to All Saints Anglican Church in Vernon, to express appreciation for his safe return.

Years later, Denison learned that the bodies of all the members of his crew, except Ian Giles, were found in Germany and buried at a military cemetery near Berlin. Giles, the flight engineer, remains unaccounted for. His name has been carved on a granite panel at the Runnymede Memorial near London, England, which honours flyers from Commonwealth countries who died during the war but have no known grave.

Although Denison's flight ended disastrously, that night other bombers went all the way to Chemnitz. *The Bomber Command War Diaries*,

Harry Denison's licence plate in 2005 explained how he descended from the sky.

written by Martin Middlebrook and Chris Everitt, says that the central and southern part of Chemnitz suffered severe fire damage on the night of March 5, 1945, and that several factories, including one that made tanks, were destroyed. The book also says that nine aircraft from the air force group to which Denison's squadron was attached crashed near their bases that night, after taking off in the icy conditions.

The raid was part of a bombing campaign called Operation Thunderclap. Near the end of the war, the western Allies concentrated their bombing flights on eastern Germany, in order to assist the Russians who were rapidly advancing from the east.

———◆———

Harry Denison was only twenty years old when he arrived home after the war. He wasn't even old enough to buy a drink in a bar.

Denison left the military to work on the family farm, later going into construction and the transportation field. He lives today in a home near North Bay, Ontario, overlooking Lake Nipissing.

He still wonders about the cause of the explosion and suspects that an Allied plane collided with NP799. He thinks his crew would have spotted a German night fighter.

Although not dwelling on the past, he drives around North Bay with a small reminder of his ordeal. The licence plate on his forest green Toyota van contains the letters "NO CHUT." It sums up the story of how he descended from the sky above Germany.

"I'm a survivor," Denison, who will be eighty-six in 2010, said when interviewed at his home. He views his wartime experiences philosophically and said he learned to take one day at a time.

6
THE GROUND WAR

Leading Aircraftsman George McHale straddled a cannon on the wing of a Typhoon fighter-bomber as he guided the pilot on a taxiing runway at the Eindhoven airbase in the Netherlands. The pilot needed McHale's help because the long nose of a Typhoon rises above the cockpit when the plane is on the ground, obscuring the pilot's view.

It was 9:20 a.m., January 1, 1945. McHale, twenty-two, had not been able to celebrate New Year's Eve. Instead, he had been working hard. An air frame mechanic with 440 Squadron of the Royal Canadian Air Force, McHale, along with a mechanic who looked after the engine, had to make sure that the Typhoon was ready to fly.

McHale, who grew up on a farm near Wood Mountain in southern Saskatchewan, knew the war was coming to an end. The Allies had, in fact, taken the Eindhoven base from the Luftwaffe as the German forces retreated to their own country.

The pilot revved the Typhoon's engine. He was ready to take off for a strafing flight on a cold but sunny morning. As McHale was about to jump off the plane, he noticed four German fighter planes roaring toward him from the opposite end of the runway. They fired cannon shells and machine-gun bullets. He could see the shells coming from the centre of the propeller of the lead aircraft, a Focke-Wulf 190.

He jumped off the wing and looked for cover. There was none. The area where the taxiing runway joined a main runway was completely open.

McHale saw a loose brick

George McHale in 1941.

on the frozen ground, and he dived behind it. Even though it was small, the brick offered him some sense of security; nevertheless, he thought his life was about to end. One bullet could kill him.

When McHale looked at the Typhoon, he saw a fire in the lower part of the fuselage. McHale noticed that the pilot was standing up in the cockpit. He had opened the canopy and was firing his handgun at the German planes. This concerned McHale. He feared that the pistol shots would make both him and the pilot targets for the German fighters.

The fighters left and circled around the base. McHale had been lucky. The shells missed him by about a metre. The only thing that hit him was an empty shell case, but it didn't injure him.

He got up, climbed onto the port wing of the Typhoon and went to the pilot. "Let's get off of here," McHale said. He noticed that the pilot had a head wound, perhaps from pieces of the Typhoon's canopy that flew off during the attack. The pilot's face was covered with blood, and he appeared to be disoriented. He was shouting at the planes. McHale took the pistol from the pilot, then helped him out of the cockpit and off the aircraft.

The German fighters attacked again. McHale and the pilot fell onto the ground as quickly as they could.

McHale was lucky again. The shells just missed him, but he knew he was still in danger. He wasn't just concerned about German aircraft firing at him; he was also concerned about the Allies' ammunition. He feared the fires in the planes would set off bombs and shells that were intended for German targets.

The Allies, not expecting the Luftwaffe to mount an offensive campaign at this point in the war, stored bombs, as well as fuel, beside the aircraft. This was more convenient, but it was also more dangerous than leaving them in a separate location far from the aircraft. As shells and bombs started exploding, McHale knew he had to seek a safer place, somewhere away from the runway.

The four fighters that flew above the runway were among dozens that attacked the base, firing at planes, hangars, and vehicles.

The Luftwaffe had chosen this morning to launch an attack called Operation Bodenplatte — meaning "ground plate" — against Allied airbases in northwest Europe. The Germans had assembled an armada of fighters to support their counteroffensive in the Ardennes region of Belgium.

The Typhoon pilot went off on his own, and McHale ran toward a field on the south side of the base. He crossed the field, stepping through partly frozen ponds, slowing him up. Coming across a deep, V-shaped drainage ditch beside a road, he slowed down to catch his breath. He decided to walk along the ditch.

As the German fighters continued to attack the base, Allied fighters in the air fought back. Smoke rose above the base from the aircraft and vehicles that the German fighters had hit.

While he was in the ditch, McHale noticed red hot fragments of bombs flying over him. He came across a corrugated metal culvert that drained into the ditch. There was no water in the culvert, only a bit of ice. He had found something that might protect him. He felt relieved, but as he got into the culvert the explosions dramatically increased. Wind from an explosion rushed into the ditch, and blew him about a metre in. McHale quickly learned to hold onto the end of the culvert as soon as he heard an explosion.

While he was in there he realized that he had cut his right knee. Apart from that, he was uninjured. The culvert had protected him.

———◆———

When no bombs had exploded for about twenty minutes, McHale left the culvert. He started walking along the ditch again, went around the base and then back into it. Most of the fires were out by that time.

McHale entered the base hospital, which wasn't damaged. A doctor examined the cut on his knee, but it wasn't too severe and he returned to work within a few days. He then went to the commander of his squadron to turn in the handgun he had taken from the pilot.

———◆———

From the Luftwaffe's perspective, the attack on the Eindhoven base was successful. In his book, *Dawn of Destruction*, Arthur Bishop calls the raid the most devastating of the entire Bodenplatte operation. He reports that the German fighters destroyed 144 Allied planes on the ground and damaged another eighty-four. Several pilots and forty members of ground crews were killed.

The Eindhoven raid, however, was costly to the Germans too. Of the seventy pilots who attacked the base, twenty-two were killed, declared missing, or became prisoners of war. These were pilots that Germany

Ian Darling

George McHale in 2007.

could not afford to lose.

Despite the Allies' casualties at Eindhoven and other bases, Operation Bodenplatte did not permanently weaken the Allied air forces. They recovered quickly and, day after day, sent aircraft over Germany to bring Adolf Hitler's Thousand Year Reich to an end.

———————◆———————

McHale left the air force shortly after the war ended, but he decided to rejoin two years later because he liked the life. During his postwar career he also looked after planes used by the United Nations to fly observers in Kashmir. He retired as a warrant officer in Transport Command, at Trenton, Ontario, in 1972. McHale, who will be eighty-eight in 2010, lives in Coquitlam, B.C.

Looking back on the Eindhoven raid, McHale realizes that luck plays a significant role in war. If he had been a few inches either to his left or right as he lay on the ground, he could have been killed.

Ground crews receive little recognition for their contribution to the war. Unlike pilots, they aren't perceived as glamorous. But the ground crews know that no pilot could fly without them, and as George McHale showed on January 1, 1945, they could be in just as much danger as a pilot in the air.

7
THE LUCKIEST GUY

Flying Officer Carl Rudyk was checking the route back to England. Rudyk, a navigator, and his crewmates on Lancaster bomber ND650 were over western Germany, near Duisburg, not far from the Dutch border. The crew had already dropped their bombs on Berlin, in eastern Germany.

Their overnight flight began on March 24, 1944. The sky was dark, but that suddenly changed. "Have a look," Flying Officer Fred Hentsch, the pilot, shouted over the intercom. Rudyk, a twenty-seven-year-old Canadian from Edmonton, left his navigator's desk and walked to the cockpit. He saw a massive wall of light. German searchlights lit the sky.

He knew that Hentsch would have trouble getting ND650 away from the lights. He might not get back to his base at Wickenby in Lincolnshire, where he was serving with the Royal Air Force's 12 Squadron.

Carl Rudyk

Carl Rudyk in 1943.

Rudyk returned to his navigator's seat. The plane flew into the lights. Hentsch started turning the bomber to the left and then the right, trying to get out of them, but anti-aircraft crews had spotted the plane. Then, Rudyk heard a loud explosion ahead of ND650. An anti-aircraft shell had exploded, sending dozens of pieces of shrapnel at the plane. Several entered the fuselage. One piece tore the flesh off the calf muscle of Rudyk's right leg.

Shrapnel also hit the fuel tanks in the aircraft's wings. Fuel spread to the fuselage where it instantly ignited. The interior of the plane burst into flames, and the sides burned like paper. Rudyk had to get out.

◆

Rudyk picked up his parachute, which was near his seat, snapped it on and started going to the lower level. As he left, he walked near Hentsch, who patted him on the shoulder. Hentsch didn't say anything because of the noise.

Despite his injured leg, Rudyk walked down the steps to the aircraft's lower level. He found that another member of the crew had already removed the cover of the escape hatch — he assumed it was Sergeant Albert Keveren, the bomb-aimer, and that he had already left. Rudyk didn't see any other members of the crew.

Because the aircraft was moving in an erratic manner, Rudyk didn't have a chance to ease his way through the hatch. He dived through, but one of his feet got caught. He was trapped.

Then the strong wind created by the moving aircraft confronted him. He struggled, and eventually his foot came loose. Rudyk was out, but the force of the wind had knocked him unconscious.

Somehow, Rudyk's hand pulled the ripcord, opening his parachute. Still unconscious, he descended into Nazi Germany.

When Rudyk woke up, he found himself lying on his back on a plowed field. The sky was dark again. The sun had not come up. He noticed that some German farmers had formed a circle around him. One of them probably saw his parachute come down. The farmers stared at him, but didn't come too close. They feared he might be armed.

Even though his right leg was injured, Rudyk felt no pain. In response to a severe injury, the human body produces adrenalin, as well as endorphins — morphinelike substances that act as natural painkillers. Rudyk felt relieved; he was alive.

The farmers brought a ladder and used it as a stretcher to take him to a nearby farmhouse. They called the local German authorities, who came to the house and took Rudyk to a hospital in the small city of Geldern.

He was taken to a room with a wounded American airman. The American was badly burned and his face was fully bandaged.

A young German doctor entered and approached Rudyk's bed. He spoke no English, but made a sawing motion with his hand. Rudyk understood what that meant. The doctor wanted to amputate the lower part of his right leg. Rudyk nodded in agreement. The doctor performed the surgery, amputating above the knee. The operation was successful — Rudyk never felt any discomfort.

The German doctor came to see his Canadian patient each day. "Guten morgen," he said, and proceeded to look after Rudyk in a professional manner. The hospital treated Rudyk and the American airman as regular patients, except that twice a day a German soldier came to the room. The soldier was friendly and smiled as he counted Rudyk and the American, who were now prisoners of war. "Eins, zwei," the soldier said — one, two. The count was rather unnecessary because the two injured flyers were in no condition to escape.

Outside the hospital, the war continued. Rudyk could hear anti-aircraft guns firing shells at Allied bombers. He could also hear German soldiers marching. The soldiers were from nearby anti-aircraft units — like the one that brought down ND650.

Rudyk's mind often wandered back to Edmonton, where his wife, Louise, lived with their son, Evan, who was only two-and-a-half years old. Rudyk knew his wife would soon receive some bad news.

———◆———

Louise Rudyk received a telegram from the air force casualty office in Ottawa, three days after her husband went on the flight to Berlin. It said that Rudyk was missing.

Several weeks later, on May 9, she received a second telegram. It said the International Red Cross had learned from German sources that Rudyk had been killed. Although the information was erroneous, Louise was devastated. She thought she was a widow who had to look after not only herself, but also young Evan.

———◆———

Rudyk's leg healed well. After a few weeks, he was able to walk with the help of crutches.

One day, a sergeant in the Luftwaffe came to Rudyk's room. The sergeant was a guard who had been assigned to escort Rudyk to Geldern's railway station. The guard did not speak English, so Rudyk did not know where he was going.

Rudyk and the guard got into a compartment in the first class carriage of a train. Two well-dressed men and a woman, who was with her son, were in the compartment. The son was a soldier who, like Rudyk, had lost a leg.

A conductor entered the compartment and became upset when he saw a Canadian airman. The conductor wanted Rudyk to sit in the carriage immediately behind the engine, because that part of the train was more vulnerable to an attack by an Allied fighter plane.

The conductor left. When he later returned, he started yelling because Rudyk was still in the carriage. Rudyk's guard stood up, getting ready to move, but the two men in the carriage told him to remain seated. The men talked to the conductor in the hallway. They apparently persuaded him to let Rudyk and his guard stay in the carriage. The two men smiled. Rudyk realized that some Germans were compassionate.

The train went through Cologne, where Rudyk could see the results of the massive Allied bombing campaign. The city was a pile of rubble.

Frankfurt, which Allied bombers had set on fire, was next. The walls of what were once buildings were black.

At about 5:00 p.m. the train stopped at the Frankfurt station. Rudyk and his guard got off. The guard left Rudyk in the middle of the station while he sought directions to his destination. Rudyk was still in the uniform in which he flew to Berlin. The station was crowded. Rudyk feared someone might seek revenge for the bombing campaign by attacking him, but no one threatened an airman with one leg. The guard returned and escorted his prisoner to Dulag Luft, the Luftwaffe's interrogation centre near Frankfurt.

———————◆———————

The next morning, Rudyk woke up to a beautiful spring day. A cuckoo made its presence known outside his window. A German officer entered Rudyk's room and sat down.

"Do you smoke," the officer said in perfect English.

"Yes I do," Rudyk replied.

The officer gave Rudyk a cigarette. He was well briefed, and knew a lot about Rudyk's squadron.

The interrogation officer started asking questions. He wanted to know about Rudyk's base and the route Allied planes took to Germany. Flying Officer Carl Rudyk, however, provided only his name, rank, and serial number, which was J23713. When Rudyk refused to provide answers, the interrogation officer took away Rudyk's cigarette, but did not threaten him.

After staying at Dulag Luft for a few days, Rudyk went by train to Stalag Luft III, a prison camp at Sagan in eastern Germany.

———————◆———————

Eventually Rudyk was taken to a hut at the camp. He heard a Canadian accent outside his window.

"Do you smoke?"

"Yes," Rudyk said.

"What brand?"

"Export As."

The man with the Canadian accent soon brought a carton of Export As. Rudyk was amazed that he could smoke the brand of cigarette he bought at home. The cigarettes came from parcels sent to the prisoners.

Rudyk wandered around on crutches, still wearing the uniform that he was shot down in. He was able to cut off and pin up the torn lower part of his right pant leg, but he had no means of washing his uniform. The Germans did not have fresh clothes to give him.

He did make a vest by sewing together scraps of uniforms, blankets, and cloth from Red Cross parcels. On the vest he embroidered the names of military bases and prison camps where he had stayed. He also embroidered, in deep red thread, two other names that reminded him of home: Louise and Evan.

To pass the time, he played a gramophone, which he acquired by trading his watch. The gramophone, however, came with only one record, Oklahoma. Rudyk heard that song over and over. Rudyk also enjoyed watching other prisoners play baseball on a sports field.

Occasionally, Focke-Wulf fighter planes came over the camp. The German pilots flew so low that the prisoners could see their faces and could tell that they were smiling. These pilots, presumably, were showing a form of wartime camaraderie. Many Luftwaffe pilots saw themselves not as Nazis, but as airmen, just as the prisoners in the camp had been.

While at the camp, Rudyk received what became known as an Errey leg. With permission from German authorities, a Canadian PoW, Lance Corporal Donovan Errey, started making artificial legs for prisoners who had lost limbs. Errey used scraps of metal. Rudyk found his artificial leg to be too uncomfortable, so he continued to walk around the camp with the help of crutches.

The guards at the camp held a roll call twice a day. The prisoners had to line up outside. Rudyk was exempt because the guards thought a prisoner with one leg would not try to escape. They permitted him to stay in his hut.

This exemption had an unintended consequence. While most of the guards were busy counting prisoners, Rudyk would place burnt-out radio tubes from clandestine radios at the camp on his window sill. He also placed a pack of cigarettes on the sill.

During the roll call, a guard who had been bribed would come by and take the tubes and the cigarettes, returning the next day with a new tube, which Rudyk would pick up. The clandestine radios enabled the prisoners to stay in touch with the world outside the prison camp.

Rudyk noticed that some items around the camp seemed odd. The beds were missing boards — every second one had been removed. Also, sand was mixed with the regular greyish soil at the campground. Rudyk didn't understand the significance of the missing boards or the sand.

In fact, they were signs that some of the prisoners had been digging tunnels. They brought the sand to the surface and spread it around, and they used the bed boards to support the walls of the tunnels.

The largest escape from Stalag Luft III occurred before Rudyk arrived at the camp. On the night of March 24 — the night of Rudyk's ill-fated flight to Berlin — two hundred men hoped to escape through a tunnel. Seventy-six men got through the tunnel and escaped before a guard discovered it. Only three managed to remain free and return to England. The Germans found the other seventy-three — the Gestapo shot fifty of them. No one mentioned the escape to Rudyk. Presumably, the prisoners who were at the camp when the men were executed found the subject too painful to discuss with a new PoW.

Ironically, Rudyk and the other airmen who participated in the raid on Berlin, 160 kilometres away, inadvertently hindered the escape. Because of the raid, the Germans imposed a blackout, turning off the electricity. The tunnel's lights went out, delaying the movement of prisoners.

On June 4, Louise Rudyk received another telegram from the air force. It said her husband was a prisoner of war. The telegram also said he had been wounded. It offered no further details. She felt overwhelming relief, even though she did not know where he was and could not correspond with him.

While at the camp, Rudyk had no way of communicating with his wife.

Life at the prison camp changed on June 6 — D-Day. The Allies had landed in Normandy, France. The prisoners throughout the camp let out a big cheer when they heard the news on a clandestine radio. The guards looked glum.

In late December, a guard told Rudyk that his name was on a list of wounded servicemen to be repatriated as part of a prisoner exchange. Rudyk was delighted. He left Stalag Luft III during the first week of January 1945. As he went through the camp gates, the other prisoners cheered him.

He was even more fortunate than he realized to be leaving at that time. Later that month, the Germans put the prisoners on a forced march through bitterly cold weather to get them away from the rapidly advancing Russian troops.

Rudyk boarded a train to Annaburg, where the Germans had set up a repatriation centre for Allied PoWs who would be exchanged for German prisoners of war.

In Edmonton, Rudyk's wife, Louise, still did not know where her husband was. She had no idea that he was about to come home.

———◆———

The repatriation centre was in a building that had been built as a military school by Frederick the Great of Prussia. The German guards permitted the prisoners at the centre to roam around. One day, some of them went to a farmhouse where they traded soap from their Red Cross parcels for onions. The prisoners brought the onions back to their building, where they got heavy black bread from their guards and made onion sandwiches. For Rudyk, this was a great treat. He had not tasted a vegetable other than turnips for a long time.

Even though they were on their way home, the prisoners were still in a war zone. While they were in their building, American planes flew overhead on a daytime bombing raid to eastern Germany. The guards ordered the men not to stand by the windows. They may have feared that the prisoners would send signals to the planes or might learn something of military value. They may also have suspected that the prisoners could become difficult to control if they knew that the Allies were able to penetrate deep into Germany.

The prisoners obeyed the order — instead of standing by the windows, they lay on the floor and found that they could still see through the windows. The prisoners were delighted with what they saw.

After a few days at Annaburg, Rudyk and other wounded prisoners boarded a train that took them to Switzerland, a neutral country. It stopped at the Swiss city of Berne.

A train going in the opposite direction was also there. It was filled with soldiers who were in a similar condition to Rudyk and his comrades. Some had lost limbs and others were blind. They were wounded German troops who were going home.

This was the prisoner exchange Rudyk had been waiting for. From then on, American officers were in charge of the train. The former prisoners were exceptionally happy. They were free.

The train left Berne and headed for the Mediterranean port of Marseilles, in France. For the servicemen, this was friendly territory.

At one station where the train stopped, they gave some cigarettes to a Frenchman standing on the station platform. He appreciated this gesture because cigarettes were in short supply. He then left the station, but soon returned with a case of wine that he passed to the men through a window. The former prisoners were pleased. French wine had not been on their prison camp menus.

A senior American officer, however, saw the wine. Realizing that the men had been wounded, he confiscated the case. "That stuff will kill you," he said. The former prisoners were deeply upset.

At Marseilles, Rudyk and the other troops boarded the *Gripsholm*, a former luxury liner. The Allies and the Germans had agreed to use the ship to exchange prisoners of war. To prevent any warship from attacking it, the *Gripsholm* was painted in the blue and yellow colours of the flag of Sweden, a neutral country. It was also well lit at night.

Rudyk could hardly believe his good fortune. At breakfast, he could eat something he hadn't had for a long time: white bread and hard-boiled eggs. The waiters kept coming back to ask if he wanted anything else. He just kept ordering more eggs.

He did have one problem, however. While still in the harbour, the *Gripsholm* gently bobbed up and down. Rudyk, who had not felt pain when his leg muscles were injured, became seasick.

The *Gripsholm* remained in Marseilles for several days while more troops came on board. On the Atlantic it sailed into rough weather, which made the thirteen-day voyage difficult for a man on crutches. The ship arrived at New York City on February 21, 1945. From the *Gripsholm*'s deck, Rudyk saw the Statue of Liberty, standing as a powerful symbol of the freedom that he and his comrades had fought for.

Unknown to Rudyk, a camera operator filmed the arrival of the repatriated troops. The film was for a newsreel to be shown at movie theatres before the main feature. In the days before television, this was one way Canadians and Americans learned what was happening in the world.

Back in Edmonton, Louise Rudyk went to see a movie with her sister, Gertrude. The newsreel was about the arrival of the *Gripsholm* in New York. She was filled with joy when she recognized one of the men on the deck. In fact, she stayed at the theatre to watch the newsreel several times. Yes, each time she recognized her husband. He was coming home.

The Canadian servicemen on the *Gripsholm* boarded a train for Montreal. A small group of women met the train as it pulled into the station there. They wanted to know if the former prisoners knew anything about their relatives or friends who were prisoners of war. Rudyk had no specific information to offer, but he did tell them that the Germans had treated him decently.

From Montreal, Rudyk took a train to Toronto. He was on his way to Christie Street Hospital, which was helping war veterans. Because the hospital had so many veterans to help, it couldn't fit Rudyk with an artificial leg at that time. He went to his home in Edmonton, returning to Toronto later in the spring. Even before he received his prosthesis, Rudyk learned to drive a car with standard transmission. He used his left leg on the clutch and brake. To control the gas, he used a hand-held lever on the steering wheel.

In Edmonton, Rudyk first worked with a blacksmith supply firm. After deciding to become a bookkeeper, he joined the federal income tax department, and subsequently moved to the Hamilton area. He retired in 1974.

In addition to their son Evan, the Rudyks had two more children, Anita and Patricia. Louise Rudyk died in 1984. In 2000, Rudyk moved to Cambridge, where Anita lives.

Despite having only one leg, Rudyk took up golf and enjoyed the game immensely. He played until he was eighty-four, twice shooting as low as seventy-six, and twice hitting a hole-in-one.

Throughout the postwar years, the onion remained Rudyk's favourite vegetable. It reminded him of the sandwiches his fellow PoWs put together at Annaburg while on their way home.

Four of Rudyk's crewmates did not return home after flak hit ND650. They are: Flying Officer Fred Hentsch, the pilot; Sergeant Robert Cringle, the flight engineer; Sergeant Eric Birch, the wireless operator; and Flying Officer Denys Wimlett, the rear gunner. The four men are buried at the Reichswald Forest War Cemetery in Germany.

As Rudyk suspected, Sergeant Albert Keveren, the bomb-aimer, did go through the front escape hatch. He walked in a westerly direction until he reached the Netherlands. The Dutch Resistance helped him, moving him into Belgium, where he stayed until the American army arrived.

Long after the war, Keveren visited Rudyk in Edmonton. The two men had lunch together and recounted what had happened after they bailed out of ND650.

Sergeant Alfred Summers, the mid-upper gunner, also got out of the plane. Rudyk never met him again, but Oliver Clutton-Brock's book about prisoners of war, *Footprints on the Sands of Time*, says Summers became a PoW in a German camp.

ND650 was one of 811 Allied aircraft participating in the raid on Berlin. In their book, *The Bomber Command War Diaries*, Martin Middlebrook and Chris Everitt report that seventy-two of those planes were lost. Bombs dropped on Berlin damaged several industries and military targets, killing about 150 people. Bombs that fell on surrounding towns and villages killed another thirty.

Rudyk, who died in 2008 at the age of ninety-one, had reservations about what he did while in the air force. In his view, he participated in a campaign that killed civilians. "It bugs the hell out of me to this day," he said in an interview at the Riverbend Place Retirement Community, in Cambridge, Ontario, a few months before he died. He admired leaders who he thought were peaceful, such as Mahatma Gandhi. "We've got a lot of learning to do," he said.

Rudyk counted his blessings. He regarded himself as lucky to have been hit only in the leg when the *In later years, Carl Rudyk moved around his retirement home on an electric scooter.*

shrapnel could have killed him; lucky to have been able to get out of the plane; lucky to have pulled the ripcord; lucky to have landed safely; lucky to have received good medical care; lucky to have been repatriated; and lucky to have survived.

"I'm just the luckiest guy in the world," Rudyk said. "There's no doubt about it."

Mathew McCarthy, Waterloo Region Record

8
THE CORPORAL'S RING

At the train station in Stafford, England, in the summer of 1941, Peter Darling looked at the gold ring that his parents had given him for his twenty-first birthday. He was with his girlfriend, Freda Mountford, whom he had met at a park in Stafford. He removed the ring from his right hand and placed it on the ring finger of his left hand, signifying an unofficial engagement.

As a corporal with the Royal Air Force's 16 Maintenance Unit in Stafford, Darling's job was to send supplies and equipment to air force bases throughout Great Britain. For security reasons, the air force had not told him where he was going. As the train left the station on that sunny, warm day, he knew only that he was going to Liverpool to board a ship. Outfitted at Liverpool with a tropical kit, he realized that his overseas destination was somewhere hot.

Next, Darling boarded the SS *Anselm* with about 1,200 servicemen. The *Anselm* had seen finer days. Once a ship that carried passengers and freight, it was pressed into service as a troop carrier during the Second World War. It was dirty, crowded, damp, and slow.

Darling had left his job as a sales representative with a small cheese company in the northern English city of Newcastle to join the Royal Air Force a week after the war started. He had heard how horrible trench warfare was during the First World War, and he thought life in the air force would be less ghastly.

Peter Darling

Peter Darling in 1940.

The *Anselm* left Liverpool on June 28, 1941. There was little for the men to do on the ship. They played cards or read in their quarters, which had previously been the ship's cargo holds, or they watched the Atlantic drift by from the main deck.

The troopship sailed in a southerly direction, part of a convoy with four other ships: HMS *Challenger*, a survey ship, and three corvettes. Small, fast escort vessels, the corvettes were required because at that point in the war, German U-boats posed a deadly threat to Allied shipping in the Atlantic.

Several days after the *Anselm* had been at sea, a note placed on a bulletin board on the main deck said the ship was out of the danger zone.

That note would have intrigued the crew of the German submarine U-96 and its captain, Lieutenant-Commander Heinrich Lehmann-Willenbrock. Through the haze of an early morning fog on July 5, the U-boat crew saw the British convoy near the Azores. The U-boat sounded the alarm, and the crew got ready for an attack.

U-96 fired four torpedoes. One struck the *Anselm's* port side. The U-boat crew feared a counterattack from the convoy and could not stay near the surface to watch. The U-boat dived.

The explosion was so powerful that the *Anselm* bounced upward before settling back in the water. The torpedo struck just below the two accommodation decks, twisting the steel inside the ship. Water rushed into the *Anselm*. Its bow dipped into the ocean; its stern started rising in the air. The ship was sinking.

Darling had been sleeping in a canvas hammock, on the first level below the main deck, when the torpedo struck. The force of the explosion threw him onto a heavy mess table that was underneath his hammock, and then onto the floor. Stunned, he lay there in pain.

The two bones in the lower part of his right leg were broken. The tibia, commonly called the shinbone, and the fibula, the slender bone beside it, were pointing sideways at a ninety-degree angle. No one was near him to help him get out.

On the main deck, men scrambled to put on life jackets and get into lifeboats. The *Challenger* sailed up to the *Anselm* and rescued the men jumping off the troopship's stern as it was rising.

Reverend Herbert Cecil Pugh, a padre from an RAF base at Bridgnorth in England, who had been asleep on the *Anselm*, came onto the main deck. Rushing around, Reverend Pugh comforted injured men and helped get the lifeboats and rafts launched. When the padre realized that a number of injured airmen were trapped below deck, he pleaded to be lowered on a rope to comfort them.

One of the men watching as Reverend Pugh made his request was Leading Aircraftman Dave Everett, who was on his way to Rhodesia, now Zimbabwe, to be trained as a pilot. He had been running on the *Anselm*'s deck with a friend, to stay trim, when the torpedo struck.

Reverend Herbert Cecil Pugh with his two sons, Geoffrey (on left) and Alastair, in Margate, England, about 1935.

Aware that going below meant certain death, the padre wanted to be with his men. "My love of God is greater than my fear of death," he said. The men on the deck lowered the padre with a rope and he went into a shattered metal staircase in front of the *Anselm*'s bridge. When he knelt to pray, the water was up to his shoulders.

Shortly afterwards, Everett jumped overboard, swam toward a life raft, and hung onto it until rescued by the *Challenger*.

As he regained full consciousness on the floor of his deck, Darling smelled smoke and gunpowder. He heard the rushing water and the screams of young men trapped in the ship. Some cried out for their mothers.

If he were going to live, he would have to get out by himself. In the dim light, he could see men climbing a set of stairs on the other side of the ship, but he could not reach the stairs because the explosion had blown off the hatches that formed a large part of the floor of each deck.

He remembered seeing a metal ladder attached to a support column on the starboard side of the hold that led to the main deck. Darling hopped toward it on his left leg. He found the ladder and started pulling himself up with his arms. He feared that his broken right leg would become caught in one of the ladder's rungs.

As he stepped on each rung, he could see more of the sky. The light from the rising sun gave him hope. Step by step, he got closer to the opening.

Finally, he reached the top and looked out. What he saw astonished him: a deserted deck. The lifeboats had gone. Darling was alone.

Two corvettes from the convoy, HMS *Petunia* and HMS *Lavender*, searched for the U-boat. The sky was cloudy, the sea was calm, and visibility was a little more than ten kilometres.

The *Petunia*, which had been on the *Anselm's* starboard side, dropped six depth charges. The *Lavender*, which had been on the port side, dropped twenty.

Despite their efforts, the crews on the two corvettes did not know if they had destroyed the U-boat.

After he looked out of the opening, Darling pulled himself onto the main deck. He hopped to a nearby railing, holding onto it to balance himself while he decided what to do. He was still alone.

Suddenly, a young member of the *Anselm's* crew, carrying life jackets in both hands, came running toward him from the stern. "Get off the ship," he shouted. "She's sinking."

"I know," said Darling, who could see that the bow was partly underwater. The young man tossed him a life jacket. The corporal put it on then slipped into the warm ocean, only to be dragged down by the swirling water. Trapped beneath the surface until he could no longer hold his breath, he started swallowing water.

The force of the water loosened the ring he had placed on his ring finger at the train station. The ring slipped over his knuckle and was about to come off, but, while desperately trying to reach the surface, he managed to push it back on his finger.

After surfacing at last, he swam as far from the *Anselm* as he could, finally coming across a long, thick piece of wood from the ship. He climbed onto it and used it like a raft. He dangled his right leg in the water to reduce the pain. Other servicemen were in the water, some on similar pieces of debris. Others were dead, their bodies floating on the surface around him.

The *Anselm*'s bow continued to fill with water, descending deeper into the ocean. The stern was completely out of the water, almost upright. A man holding onto a railing at the stern screamed and fell into the ocean. Then, only twenty-two minutes after the torpedo struck, the *Anselm* went straight down into the Atlantic.

Shortly after, a small motorboat from one of the ships in the convoy came up to the piece of wood. "Come on board," a man said, but with his broken leg, Darling could not climb into the boat. The crew pulled him aboard and laid him down on the side of the boat. He was given a shot of morphine, and then he lost consciousness.

The *Petunia* and the *Lavender* ceased dropping depth charges when they came close to survivors who were still in the water, waiting to be rescued by the *Challenger* and the third corvette in the convoy, HMS *Starwort*.

The corvettes gave up their search for the U-boat three hours after the attack. The convoy resumed its southerly voyage, leaving behind 254 men who had just died in the Atlantic.

———————◆———————

After the attack, U-96 moved north in a zigzag pattern. The barrage of depth charges had damaged it. The submarine was leaking, and the crew had to work hard to pump out the water. The U-boat had to return to its base for repairs.

The submarine's log book reveals that after they had survived the counterattack, the young German sailors made snide jokes about the British depth charges missing them.

They were, in fact, lucky to be alive. The Royal Navy's Monthly Anti-Submarine Report for September 1941 says the *Petunia* and the *Lavender* apparently acted independently when they hunted for the U-boat. It suggests that if the corvettes had properly coordinated their counterattack, they might have destroyed the submarine.

———————◆———————

When Darling woke up, he found himself under an awning on the deck of one of the ships in the convoy. He also learned that the ship had no medical facilities. Other rescued men chatted with him as he lay on his back, his right leg still at a sharp angle. They told him about a padre who had gone below deck as the *Anselm* was sinking. They told him that no one had seen the padre after that.

The ship and the convoy sailed on, cruising through calm waters and under sunny skies. After a few days, a larger vessel came alongside the ship. Darling was strapped on a Robertson stretcher: a stretcher made with a bamboo frame that was lifted by crane. Despite his fears that the cable holding the stretcher could snap, he was hoisted through the air, transferred to the larger vessel, and taken to its sick bay.

A doctor quickly took charge with the help of two strong assistants. The doctor wanted to realign the bones in Darling's lower right leg so that they would graft in a vertical position. He attached wires and weights to the corporal's leg. Each day, he adjusted them so that the bones gradually returned to their proper position.

The assistants' job was to hold Darling down while the doctor performed this painful procedure. The doctor had no anesthetic to give. Instead, he offered a cloth-covered rope to bite.

After another week of sailing, the ship docked at Freetown in Sierra Leone, then a British colony. An ambulance took Darling to a military hospital. Soon after he arrived, doctors operated on his leg, putting it in a cast. His ward was filled with soldiers in the British Army who had also been on the *Anselm*. One patient was a paraplegic, injured when a lifeboat being lowered crashed into another.

After a few days, some of the other survivors from the *Anselm* visited the patients in the hospital, and one arranged to send a telegram to Darling's parents in Newcastle asking them to send him £2. For security reasons, nothing could be said about the *Anselm* or what had happened to him.

Relieved to learn that their son was alive, Percy and Maud Darling were later shocked to receive a telegram from the air ministry. It informed them that their son had been killed.

Even after further correspondence assured them that he was alive, they still did not know what had happened. In one letter, Darling's father asked him if a German submarine had torpedoed his troopship. Because military censors would not permit him to give a proper response, Darling answered by saying, "Dad's idea of the tin fish was very good."

After he spent the £2 his parents sent, he asked an army paymaster at the hospital if he could arrange for an air force paymaster to come to the ward to provide him with some money. A few days later, an air force officer arrived and asked him if he was Corporal Darling. The corporal assured him that he was. The officer then asked Darling to state his serial number, which he did: 936943. The officer looked him in the eye and said, "Corporal, you're dead."

Realizing that the report of the corporal's death was rather inaccurate, the officer put him on the payroll. Despite needing a second operation, his leg gradually healed. By November, he was walking with a limp. By Christmas, the hospital discharged him, and he was given a new uniform and cap badge to replace the items that went down with the *Anselm*.

Shortly afterwards, Darling was flown to Takoradi, in what is now Ghana, but was then the British colony known as Gold Coast. In Takoradi, he resumed working in the equipment section of an air force base.

Because of his injury, Darling was exhausted at the end of a regular work day. A medical board decided that he should return to Britain. This trip would also be by ship. Although apprehensive at the thought of another wartime voyage on the Atlantic, he was glad to be going home.

———————◆———————

In 1943, Darling was promoted to sergeant, and in April of that year he placed a wedding ring on Freda's finger. He continued to work at various RAF bases in England until his unit was posted to Belgium, in January 1945. By then the Allies were advancing toward victory. He remained in Belgium until May 1945, when he returned to air force bases in England. After being demobilized in March 1946, he joined his family's grocery business in Newcastle.

———————◆———————

The German navy retired U-96 from active duty in 1943 and used it for training purposes. One of Germany's most famous submarines, U-96 provided the setting for Lothar-Gunther Buchheim's novel, *Das Boot* or *The Boat*, which was subsequently turned into a movie.

In an introductory note, the book mentions that 30,000 of the 40,000 German sailors who served on U-boats during the Second World War did not return home.

The captain of U-96, Heinrich Lehmann-Willenbrock, was one of the German sailors who did return home. He survived the war.

———————◆———————

Peter Darling's ordeal at sea did not stop him from taking a ship across the Atlantic when he immigrated to Canada in 1956, along with Freda and his children — my brother John and me.

Darling, who will be ninety-one in 2010, lives in a retirement home in Waterloo, Ontario. He started talking about his experience on the *Anselm* only in recent years. He wanted his grandchildren to know what war is really like.

He also had several telephone conversations with Dave Everett, the leading aircraftman who watched the padre go below deck. Everett, who lived in Wolverhampton, England, died in 2007.

Peter Darling at a billiard table in 2008.

Reverend Pugh was posthumously awarded the George Cross for gallantry in 1947. The citation said that, "He had every opportunity of saving his own life but, without regard to his own safety and in the best tradition of the Service and of a Christian Minister, he gave up his life for others."

While discussing his ordeal on the *Anselm*, Peter Darling said his determination to get out of the ship, and then to survive while floating in the Atlantic, came from his desire to see his future wife, Freda. "I had someone waiting for me," he said.

A widower since Freda died in 1996, he still wears the ring that almost slipped away on July 5, 1941.

9
THE FOG OF WAR

On August 9, 1941, Pilot Officer Richard Gilman was escorting a plane in heavy fog and strong winds. The plane carried an important passenger. Based at Castletown, Scotland, Gilman and the other Spitfire pilots in the Royal Air Force's 124 Squadron, as well as fighter pilots from two other squadrons, did not know the identity of the passenger. They just knew that they had to escort the plane from Inverness to the Orkney Islands, just off Scotland's northeast coast.

The worse the weather became, the closer Gilman brought his Spitfire to the plane on his starboard side. Despite the fog, Gilman had to keep watching the plane.

The passenger pulled back a curtain covering a window. Gilman could see him well. He was wearing an air force uniform adorned with medals, and he had an apprehensive look on his face, which was understandable because his plane and Gilman's Spitfire were only about ten metres apart. A collision could easily occur in the turbulent air.

No collision occurred, which was good for Gilman, who was born in Vancouver but grew up in England after his family left Canada. It was also good for Great Britain because the passenger was King George VI.

—◆—

A few months later, on November 24, 1941, Gilman, who was only nineteen, had to fly again in bad weather. By then his squadron was at Biggin Hill, in south London.

He and the other pilots had been woken up at 5:00 a.m., given a good breakfast, and briefed about their flight. They were to fly to the French coast to protect a group of British commandos who had staged a brief raid in France. They were to attack any enemy aircraft that threatened the commandos' boats as they returned to England.

After the briefing, the pilots went to their Spitfires, which were dispersed around the air base. They sat in their cockpits, waiting to be told when they could take off. The weather was dreadful. The Spitfires were surrounded by mist, and pelted with rain and sleet.

Richard Gilman

Richard Gilman in 1941.

Gilman felt cold and miserable. He also felt apprehensive because at that point in the war, the Allied pilots defending the south of England had suffered heavy casualties.

After waiting about an hour and a half, Gilman and the rest of his squadron were finally airborne. The weather over the English Channel was no better. The grey sea blended with the mist and the clouds.

Flying at about 1,000 feet (300 metres) Gilman could hardly see the French coast, let alone pick out any of the boats that the Spitfires were supposed to protect. As he got closer to the coast, he did see something in the Channel. He might have spotted the commandos' boats or he might have seen fishing vessels. He couldn't tell.

No one is going to attack the commandos in this miserable weather, Gilman thought to himself.

The squadron decided to return to Biggin Hill, but because of the poor weather, the Spitfires had flown off course. They were getting low on fuel. At one point, Gilman noticed that his Spitfire, which could carry about a hundred gallons of fuel, had only five gallons left.

Squadron Leader Raymond Duke-Woolley wanted to bring the Spitfires down at the earliest opportunity. He spotted a place to land near the Channel. It was the Shoreham airfield, near Brighton. "Emergency landing," he said to the pilots on his radio.

Gilman felt relieved. He wanted to land as soon as possible. He quickly lowered his wheels. As they came down, the pilots had to move the control column in the cockpit to the left to raise the aileron on the port wing, and push the left rudder pedal to control the tail. As they did that, the pilots were supposed to watch the plane in front of them and to their port side. They had to leave some distance between their aircraft and the plane they were intensely watching.

This was the strict procedure pilots were to follow when landing, designed to prevent planes from colliding. But Flight Lieutenant Jaroslav Kulhanek, a Czech pilot flying on Gilman's starboard side, had little experience making emergency landings in a Spitfire because he had just joined the squadron. He didn't know he was too close to Gilman. Suddenly, without warning, Kulhanek's Spitfire struck Gilman's plane. Before he realized what had happened, Gilman's Spitfire was going down and twisting slightly to the left.

He had no time to bail out. The ground seemed to rush toward him. He could see a hedge and a hut that were on the edge of the airfield. As he came down, Gilman felt peaceful. He thought of his older brother, Sergeant Pilot Jack Gilman, who had been killed with his crew that summer when his Whitley bomber crashed in England, after a German night fighter attacked it. Gilman was particularly close to his brother. They had lived in the same room and played sports together. Gilman thought Jack must have experienced something similar to what was happening to him.

The commandos whom Gilman and the other pilots were supposed to protect were on their way back to England, after leaving the Houlgate area of Normandy, France. They were members of the British army's No. 9 commando unit. The goal of the ninety men on the raid was to attack German artillery guns near Houlgate.

They were not successful. In his book, *The Raiders: The Army Commandos 1940–46*, Robin Neillands says the commandos used several landing craft, but in the dark one went to the wrong beach. Those commandos who did land in the right area had trouble climbing the cliffs near the beach. Rain turned the surface of the cliffs into slippery, wet clay. The commandos didn't have enough time to get to the German guns. One commando was wounded during the raid, but all men returned to England.

The wreckage from Gilman's Spitfire was spread over a wide area. The damage was so severe that apparently no one at the airfield bothered to send an ambulance — they didn't think that a pilot could survive such a crash.

However, some soldiers manning anti-aircraft guns were near the wreckage. They found the pilot, unconscious but still breathing, and called an ambulance.

Gilman was taken to Shoreham Hospital. His right leg had multiple fractures, his right arm was also broken, and he had lost all of his teeth after the microphone at the end of his oxygen mask rammed into his mouth when the plane crashed.

As Gilman lay on his back, a nurse who was behind him spoke in a warm, encouraging voice. "Hang on, hang on," she said while she held his left hand.

"This will hurt," a doctor said as he straightened Gilman's twisted right leg.

Later that day an ambulance transferred him to Princess Mary's RAF Halton Hospital, in Buckinghamshire near London. It was a bumpy ride; Gilman could feel the edges of his broken bones rubbing against one another. At the hospital doctors placed him in a cast that covered his upper body and right leg.

———————◆———————

Kulhanek, the Czech pilot, was slightly injured when he crash-landed, but he flew again. He died later in the war when a German fighter shot his plane down over the Calais area of France, on March 13, 1942.

———————◆———————

Gilman gradually recovered at the Halton hospital. He ate his first solid food again on Christmas Day, and after a few more months he was taking small steps with the aid of crutches.

In the spring of 1942, an officer came around the hospital looking for six wounded airmen to attend a national event on April 23, but he didn't say what the event was. Gilman was selected to be one of the six.

Gilman, who was still using crutches, and the others were taken by truck to a railway station where they boarded a train for London. Another truck took the men to the Royal Albert Hall, London's famed concert hall. When they arrived, they found that the *Daily Express*, one of Britain's main newspapers, was sponsoring a massive pageant entitled Battle for Freedom. It was St. George's Day, the day on which England celebrates its patron saint who, legend says, slew a dragon with a lance. The newspaper staged the pageant to honour the men and women who were fighting the dragon in Germany that threatened Great Britain and the democratic world.

Hundreds of men and women in uniform marched into the hall. Troops carried flags of all the Allied countries. Commandos put on a performance with bayonets and Tommy guns.

Laurence Olivier, the famous actor, gave a rousing speech: "We will attack. We will smite our foes. We will conquer."

Winston Churchill was there. Spotlights focused on the prime minister when an announcer introduced him. The audience cheered and clapped. Churchill acknowledged the applause by displaying his V for victory sign with one hand, while he held a cigar in his other.

The announcer introduced veterans of the First World War who had won the Victoria Cross. The audience applauded them, too.

Then the announcer mentioned a group of flyers. Gilman looked around to see where they were. Much to his surprise, the spotlights stopped at his box. The audience didn't just clap, they gave the airmen a standing ovation. Gilman and the other airmen were astounded. Later that evening, people in the audience approached the airmen to give them cigars, chocolate bars, and even money.

By late spring, Gilman was convalescing at an RAF hospital set up in the Palace Hotel at Torquay, in Devon on the English Channel. On June 7, Gilman was enjoying a sunny Sunday afternoon away from the hospital by taking a trip on a tour bus. He had just got off the bus at the promenade near Torquay's harbour when he spotted several German fighter planes. He relaxed when he realized that they were flying toward the Channel, away from England. He became alarmed, however, when he saw them turn around and start flying back to Torquay. Gilman knew what was about to happen. "Get these people into a shelter," he shouted.

There were no military targets in the area, but the German fighters were getting ready to attack civilians in an attempt to lower the morale of the British people. The German fighters fired their machine guns at the promenade as the passengers from the bus, many of whom were older women, ran to an air raid shelter. Gilman scurried to the shelter as quickly as a man on crutches could travel. The fighters also dropped bombs.

A report at the Torquay Library reveals that four Messerschmitt 109 fighter planes participated in the raid. Seven people in the city were killed.

In late 1942, Gilman returned to the Biggin Hill base for a social visit. Without realizing that Gilman was not supposed to be flying, a flight sergeant with 124 Squadron asked him if he wanted a plane. He couldn't turn down the offer. "We'll have one ready for you in no time," the flight sergeant said.

Gilman was pleased to be back in a cockpit, but he also felt apprehensive. During the flight he realized he was not medically ready to fly the fast Spitfires.

Starting in 1943, he served as a pilot instructor, giving lectures, flying navigational exercises, and towing targets for student pilots to practise aiming machine guns at.

After the war, Gilman became a teacher and went to East Africa to develop secondary schools. He came back to Canada in 1952, accepting a teaching position at an independent school in Hamilton. He later switched to the public school system, and became a principal and superintendent.

Now retired, Gilman lives in St. Catharines. "Life was exceedingly precarious," he said when thinking back to his days as a Spitfire pilot. "It was also exciting." Gilman regards himself as exceedingly fortunate to have survived.

Indeed, Gilman had good reason to feel apprehensive as he waited at Biggin Hill to take off for the French coast on November 24, 1941. Norman L. R. Franks' book, *Royal Air Force Fighter Command Losses of the Second World War*, reveals that thirty-nine fighter pilots died that month.

For many years, Gilman felt he had been cheated out of an interesting experience: he had not been able to bail out of his Spitfire on that misty November morning. Gilman decided that he still wanted to make a parachute jump. To celebrate his eightieth birthday in 2002, Gilman made a tandem leap from a plane with Mic Sweeney, an instructor at Skydive Burnaby, a parachuting company in Wainfleet, near Lake Erie.

The weather was fine. There was no mist or fog. This time, Gilman landed safely.

Richard Gilman

To celebrate his eightieth birthday in 2002, Richard Gilman made a parachute jump with Mic Sweeney at Skydive Burnaby in Wainfleet, Ontario.

10
THE LAST TRAINING FLIGHT

Warrant Officer Wally Loucks was waiting for Morse code messages from the Royal Canadian Air Force base at Dishforth in Yorkshire, England. Loucks, who was from the Hiawatha Indian reserve near Peterborough, was in what he called his office, the radio room of Halifax bomber LK930. He had his earphones on, ready to decipher messages that might say his aircraft should take a different course or go to a different target.

Loucks and his crew were on what was called a "nickel raid." This was a training flight during which they flew toward the French coast to drop strips of aluminum foil known as "window." The foil would create the impression that many Allied bombers were in the area, in order to confuse German radar units.

It was March 21, 1944. This flight was supposed to be the crew's last training trip before they went on flights to Germany, flights that were expected to be dangerous.

LK930 had been flying for several hours when Loucks heard the plane's call letters on his Morse code receiver. He listened carefully. The message said the crew should return to the Dishforth base, but it gave no explanation, no hint of a problem.

Loucks, who was twenty-one, was happy to go back to the base. By returning, the crew would be less likely to encounter German flak guns or night fighters. Loucks relayed the message on the intercom to the pilot, Sergeant Ray Collver, and the rest of the crew: Pilot

Wally Loucks in 1941.

Officer Ralph Pilkington, the navigator; Sergeant Russell Peel, the bomb-aimer; Sergeant Russ Pym, the flight engineer; Sergeant Bill Andrew, the mid-upper gunner; and Sergeant Carl Starnes, the rear gunner.

Collver, the pilot, was a farm boy from Wellandport in the Niagara Peninsula, who had been a student minister with the Presbyterian Church of Canada before becoming a pilot. He turned LK930 to the starboard side. Pilkington, the navigator, gave Collver the directions to return to England.

On their way back, Pym, the flight engineer, spotted an oil leak on the outer starboard engine, but at night he couldn't see it well. The plane continued on its flight.

Ray Collver

Ray Collver in 1944.

While flying over the English city of Nottingham, Collver remembered that Starnes, the rear gunner, had just become engaged to a girl who lived there. "We're over Nottingham, Carl, if you want to bail out," he said jokingly. Collver felt close to his crew and he regarded them as almost like brothers.

Collver expected to land in Dishforth in about twenty minutes. After five minutes, however, he heard a terrific noise coming from the outer starboard engine. On his instrument panel he noticed that the engine was racing, causing severe vibrations. At first Collver felt shock, which quickly turned to fear. "Be sure you've got your parachutes on in case I have to give the order to bail out," he said on the intercom.

Collver pressed the button on his instrument panel to switch off the engine and "feather" the propeller. When feathered, the propeller blade would be turned to reduce wind resistance. The vibrations would then cease and the plane could fly almost normally, although at a slower speed.

After another five minutes, Collver and Pym, the flight engineer, thought they had almost succeeded. The noise and the vibrations were ceasing, but at that moment the inner starboard engine started racing and vibrating, and then both engines were racing and vibrating. The plane shook violently. The fuselage started twisting and grinding. Metal flakes fell like snow in the bomber. The aircraft squealed like a wild beast.

Collver knew LK930 was doomed. He didn't even bother to ask Loucks to send a Mayday message because no one could possibly help. "Bail out," he shouted. "Hurry, hurry, hurry."

Collver wanted the crew to leave through the front escape hatch so that he would know when everyone had left. Only then would he leave.

Peel, the bomb-aimer, removed the hatch door and slipped out of the plane. Pilkington went next, but just as he was leaving the aircraft dropped. Pilkington's head came back above the hatch before he departed a second time.

"I've got to get out of here," Loucks said to himself as he saw Pilkington's head come back. As he got ready to go through the hatch, Loucks motioned with his arms to Andrew, the mid-upper gunner, to hurry up. Andrew didn't appear to be rushing. He may not have realized the urgent need to leave the aircraft because he may not have been plugged into the intercom.

Loucks knew the aircraft was low so he pulled the ripcord of his parachute as soon as he saw the tail light of the plane fly over him.

◆

Collver was aware that Peel, Pilkington, and Loucks had left. He also knew that he hadn't seen Pym, Starnes, or Andrew. He turned around for a few seconds, but couldn't see anyone getting ready to leave. When he looked at his instrument panel again, he realized LK930 was totally out of control. It was diving and turning erratically. He pulled the control column toward him, levelling the plane.

LK930 was losing altitude quickly. Collver, however, couldn't see the ground. It was a dark night, and England was under a total blackout.

The pilot checked his speed. LK930 was flying at 180 miles per hour, (290 kilometres per hour). Unknown to Collver, the aircraft flew around a grove of trees that he couldn't see. Suddenly, with a loud bang, LK930 hit the ground, skidded across a field, plowed through a potato clamp — a pile of potatoes covered with soil that were being stored through the winter — and stopped on the road between the villages of Scarcliffe and Palterton, in Derbyshire in England's East Midlands. Flames erupted around the aircraft's port wing.

———————◆———————

Because LK930 was at a low altitude when he bailed out, Wally Loucks was in the air for only a short time. In the dark night, he couldn't see the ground. He landed on a hill, jolting his back.

A few seconds later, Loucks saw flames about three kilometres away. He knew they were coming from LK930.

Suspecting no one on the plane had survived, and unable to bear looking at the aircraft, he started walking up the hill, away from the crash site. He needed to seek shelter. He found climbing the hill to be difficult. He turned around and left his parachute, crossed a few fields and fences, finally coming to a house on a lane. He knocked on the door.

A woman opened the upstairs window. Fearing that Loucks was a German, she refused to let him in. She told him to continue walking down the lane to a Home Guard station.

Loucks continued. He found the station, which was really just a shed. He knocked on the door. An older man with a rusty rifle responded.

"Who goes there?" the guard asked.

"A friend, Canadian," Loucks replied.

"This has never happened to me before," the guard said. "I don't know what to do."

Loucks advised the guard to call the air force, but, since neither had the phone number, he suggested the guard call the local police department.

The police chief arrived and took Loucks to hospital. The chief later went to the hill where Loucks had landed, found his parachute, and returned it to the air force.

———————◆———————

Ralph Pilkington and Russell Peel both successfully parachuted out of LK930. Peel landed in a field and was picked up by a bus the next day. Pilkington's parachute became entangled in a lamppost after he landed, but he was safe.

———————◆———————

When LK930 hit the ground, Collver's face and head were severely cut. His flight jacket was covered with blood and he was dazed.

Trained to escape quickly from a plane, he pulled the pin that kept his safety harness around him and he reached above himself to open the cockpit escape hatch. He scrambled through the hatch, jumped onto the port wing, and then to the ground. Surrounded by fire, he had only one way out: to go through the flames. Acting instinctively, he walked through a wall of fire. When clear of the flames, he could hear the screams of his crewmates who were trapped. He could do nothing to help them.

Some nearby residents came to the aircraft and found the pilot groaning from his injuries. Collver asked them to leave him and go to the plane because his crewmates were still inside.

A policeman arrived and saw that Collver was close to the fire. He was sitting on a fuel tank that had fallen off the aircraft. The policeman moved him away.

A bus came along, but couldn't continue its route because the aircraft blocked the road. The driver turned the bus around and took the pilot to Mansfield Hospital.

———————◆———————

George Calow, thirty-four, and his brother, Albert, thirty, were asleep in their house in Palterton, about half a mile from the plane. The crash woke them. George ran to the aircraft while his brother went to get a car and more assistance.

The elder brother arrived at the crash site and could see an airman inside. He entered the plane through a hatch and approached Starnes, the rear gunner. Starnes' clothes were on fire and his feet were trapped in the wreckage.

Albert arrived and squeezed through a crack in the fuselage. The two brothers removed their coats and wrapped them around Starnes, extinguishing the flames. They also used their caps to put out other fires.

The brothers managed to free the flyer and took him out of the plane.

The fires burned the hands of both brothers, but Albert Calow managed to drive Starnes to Chesterfield Royal Hospital. Starnes, however, died of his injuries. The two other flyers, Sergeant Bill Andrew and Sergeant Russ Pym, died in the plane.

At Mansfield Hospital doctors treated Collver's cuts. The fire singed his hair, eyebrows, and uniform, but not his skin. While he was at the hospital, a local resident who had seen the plane come down visited him. The man told Collver that his aircraft had been headed straight for the trees moments before it skirted them and then crashed.

Collver was told he may have to remain in hospital for two months. He was also told that his injuries might prevent him from flying again. In fact, he left the hospital after only two weeks and resumed flying after two months.

Loucks, who was taken to King's Mill Hospital in Mansfield, suffered from shock and a badly shaken back. The medical staff also noticed that he had an unrelated illness: the mumps.

All four flyers who survived the crash of LK930 returned to active service with different crews and squadrons. All completed their tours and returned to Canada.

Shortly after the war ended, King George VI invited George and Albert Calow to Buckingham Palace. The king presented them with the British Empire Medal for their attempt to save the trapped airmen.

When he returned to Canada, Collver wanted to buy a farm. He loved farm life, having grown up on a farm that raised Ayrshire cattle. In the fall of 1945, he went to see a farm in the Bracebridge area of Ontario. On his way back to Wellandport, his train stopped at Union Station in Toronto.

While walking around, he looked up and realized he was at the headquarters of the Presbyterian Church of Canada at 100 Adelaide St. W. He entered the building with the intention of informing the church that he did not want to return to the ministry. He spoke to Reverend William Cameron, secretary of the church's board of missions. Cameron remembered sending Collver, as a student minister, to a church in Cranberry Portage in Manitoba. Collver told Cameron about his intention of purchasing a farm.

Wally Loucks in 2007.

Cameron didn't pressure Collver, but merely said there were so many places that needed a pastor. "Find me a place and I'll go," Collver said impulsively, much to his own surprise.

Ray Collver and his wife, Blanche, went to Meath Park in Saskatchewan. After a few months, Collver started wondering if God spared his life in the crash to enable him to preach. As time went by, he became more convinced that this is what happened. He believed this view even more strongly after he returned to Palterton, long after the war, and saw the grove of trees LK930 had flown around.

In 1962, Collver left Canada to preach in a church in Minnesota. Collver, who will be ninety-one in 2010, lives in Lewisville, Texas, and remains active in his church.

Ray Collver

Ray Collver and his wife Blanche, about 1985.

Wally Loucks returned to Toronto and worked in the hardware business. In 1972, he set up A-Z Technical Bldg. Systems Inc., which constructs steel buildings. Loucks, who will be eighty-eight in 2010, still puts in a full day at his office, which is in his condominium unit in Etobicoke.

Like Collver, Loucks has been back to the site of the crash. He returned in 1985, and had a chance to talk to Albert Calow, one of the brothers who tried to save the trapped airmen.

Loucks is still not certain whether LK930's problems were caused by flak or mechanical failure.

Long after the war, Russell Peel, the bomb-aimer, told Loucks that he had a conversation with an engineering sergeant, Buddy Lawson, who was at the Dishforth base on March 21, 1944. He thought LK930 was not safe to fly. Apparently, a senior officer at the base overruled the sergeant. To this day, Loucks wonders if the aircraft was called back because someone belatedly realized the plane should not have been in the air. Loucks will never know if three of his crewmates — Russ Pym, Carl Starnes, and Bill Andrew — died because an officer approved a flight that should never have occurred.

11
A RIDE WITH FIFI

Flying Officer Gordon Stacey was at the navigator's table of his Halifax bomber, LL243, when shells ripped into the body of the plane. He thought they sounded like bees buzzing around a hive.

"Crew report," Flying Officer Gerry Maffre, the pilot, said in a calm, professional voice on the intercom. He wanted to find out if the shells had killed or injured any of his crew.

"OK, skipper," Stacey said. Other members of the crew said they were fine, but the tail gunner, Sergeant Vince Cownden, did not respond.

"You better go back to see how Vince is," Maffre said to Sergeant Alan Fuller, the flight engineer. The pilot also told the crew to prepare to abandon the aircraft. Fuller was getting ready to check on the tail gunner when Sergeant Bob Meek, the mid-upper gunner, yelled out,

Gordon Stacey

Gordon Stacey in 1942.

"Fighter, fighter below!"

More shells burst into the bomber.

Stacey went up a couple of steps to the cockpit, to see if the pilot had any instructions. "Get the hell out of here," Maffre said. On his way down, Stacey heard Flying Officer Johnny Arscott, the bomb-aimer, cry out, "I'm hit."

Only Stacey heard him because by then the intercom wasn't working. Stacey helped Arscott to get up. "Are you all right, Johnny?" Stacey asked.

"Get out!" Arscott shouted.

Stacey, who had just put on his parachute, removed the escape hatch door on the floor of the bomber, got out and pulled the ripcord. He immediately wondered if he had made the right decision. To him, leaving the plane was like leaving home.

As he came down, Stacey looked up. He could see that the starboard wing was on fire. Moments later, at about 1:30 a.m., on April 28, 1944, he saw LL243 crash to the ground.

◆

Gordon Stacey grew up in Toronto and had been intrigued by airplanes ever since he was a young boy and his father, Austin Stacey, took him to Leaside Airport on a Sunday afternoon. A civilian pilot of a Curtiss JN4, a First World War biplane, had asked his father if he would like to go for a ride. He turned down the offer and let young Gordon go instead. That was his first flight. He was thrilled.

Stacey later studied aviation engineering at Central Technical School, and after graduating he went to work as a mechanic at Patterson and Hill Aircraft, at Barker Airport in Toronto.

In December 1941, shortly after the Japanese attacked Pearl Harbor, Stacey realized that Britain and the Allies were in serious trouble. He decided to join the Royal Canadian Air Force.

LL243 had been based with the air force's 434 Squadron at Croft Spa in Yorkshire, England. The crew had been participating in a raid on the railway yards at Montzen, a town in eastern Belgium. The Allies had targeted the yards because they were on a main rail line between Germany and France. With the invasion of Normandy in France just weeks away, the Allies were attacking transportation centres to stop Nazi Germany from sending reinforcements to France.

As Stacey gently descended through the cool spring air, he could see German searchlights seeking out the Allied aircraft. He could also hear the Allied bombs exploding. After about ten minutes, he came down on a freshly plowed field, slightly injuring his left knee as he landed.

Because the borders of Belgium, Germany, and the Netherlands converge near Montzen, Stacey was not sure which country he was in. He was sure, however, that he wanted to get as far away as possible from where he had landed. Even if he were in the Netherlands or Belgium, German troops occupying those countries would be searching for flyers shot down during the night.

Stacey rolled up his parachute and buried it in a pile of manure. He used his hands to scoop out a hole for it. As a souvenir he kept the metal ring at the end of his ripcord.

He wanted to go in a southwesterly direction, away from Germany. As a navigator, Stacey knew how to use the stars to guide him. He looked up, found the Big Dipper and the North Star, and started walking, looking over his right shoulder from time to time to keep the North Star behind him.

Walking as quietly as possibly, he went through fields, and over fences and hedges. Some of the hedges had barbed wire in them, which ripped his trousers.

During the night, Stacey became thirsty and he started looking for a clear stream. As the sun came up, he came across a spring near a hill. He remembered an aunt on a farm in Canada telling him that if a stream contained watercress, the water would be suitable to drink. He checked the stream; it contained watercress.

For an airman whose plane had been shot down, who feared all his crewmates were dead, who didn't know where he was or if the local residents would help him, the discovery of a stream with watercress served as a good omen. He began to believe he might survive.

Near the stream, Stacey spotted a wooden shack that was about 200 metres from a farmhouse. He went into it, ate some of the Horlick's chocolate tablets from the emergency ration kit he carried, and went to sleep on a bunk.

Stacey woke up in the afternoon. He could see farm workers in the nearby fields, and he kept watching them and listening, in case anyone approached the shack. No one did. Because he had participated in extensive training sessions on surviving in a foreign land, Stacey did not feel particularly nervous.

He ate more of the nutritious Horlick's tablets, and mended his trousers with a needle and thread that were in his emergency kit. He checked the silk maps of several European countries that he carried, but they did not provide enough details to help him. He cut down his heavy flying boots to make them appear to be regular shoes, and he refilled his water bottle.

Despite his strained knee, Stacey was ready to resume his trek as soon as the sun went down. He continued walking in a southwesterly direction, taking a path through a wooded area.

After he walked for about half an hour, the ground became clear. The trees had been cut. He noticed trenches in the ground.

Although Stacey didn't realize their significance, they formed the border between the Netherlands and Belgium. He had parachuted into the Netherlands and was now walking into Belgium. Soon he was back in farm country, crossing small hedges that separated fields.

About midnight, he came across a road with ditches and hedges on both sides. He suddenly heard heavy footsteps, and crouched behind a small hedge. He watched through the low branches. At first, he could see only the glow of two cigarettes. Then he realized the cigarettes were held by men wearing uniforms. The two men spoke in a guttural style that Stacey assumed was German. They walked closer and closer toward him, finally stopping only six metres away. He saw that they carried rifles, while he carried no weapon at all.

Unknown to Stacey, two other members of his crew had successfully bailed out of LL243 before it crashed onto a farm at Gulpen, in the southeast Netherlands.

Fuller, the flight engineer, landed in a field in the Netherlands and walked to a village. In the village a man had shone a flashlight on him, realized that he was an Allied airman and shook his hand.

Speaking in broken English, the man told Fuller to wait for a bus that stopped in the village. He boarded the bus when it came and travelled about thirty kilometres. A passenger told Fuller to leave the bus and go to a particular house, which he did.

Someone on the bus, however, informed the Dutch police, who went to the house. The police turned Fuller over to the German authorities. He then became a prisoner of war, spending time at various camps.

Arscott, the bomb-aimer, also bailed out. He parachuted into a herd of cows, hitting one as he landed. The startled cow mooed. Arscott was concerned that the noise would draw attention to him.

He removed his parachute, but he couldn't walk because of his injured leg. While crawling on his hands and knees, he tried to calm the cows by saying "ssshh" as he crossed their field.

Arscott came to a road where he rested. Members of the Dutch Resistance happened to walk by and offered to help him. They arranged for a doctor to treat his injuries and found him safe houses to stay in.

All other members of the crew — Maffre, Meek, Cownden, and Flight Sergeant Willie Snow, the wireless operator — died when the plane crashed.

———◆———

The two German soldiers sat down on the road and each lit another cigarette. They laughed, apparently telling each other jokes. They were completely unaware that an Allied airman could hear everything they said, even if he couldn't understand a word. They finished their cigarettes, then continued walking down the road.

Feeling relieved, Stacey stood up, crossed the road, and walked back onto farmland. Thirsty and hungry, he decided to start looking for local residents who he hoped would help him.

The sun rose. He started to approach several farmhouses, but when he heard dogs barking he decided not to get any closer. He felt safer approaching houses that didn't have a dog to warn the owner that a stranger was on the property.

Finally, Stacey came to a small hamlet and saw a two-storey, red brick house that was rather isolated. No dog barked. He went immediately to the back of the house, shooed some goats away, and hid between two buildings in the farmyard. From there he could see the house, but he didn't think anyone would see him. Within a few minutes an elderly woman came out with a stool and a couple of buckets to milk the goats. Realizing that she was by herself, Stacey decided to approach her. Still wearing his battle uniform, he stepped out from between the two buildings and pointed to the word "Canada" that was embroidered in sky-blue thread on the shoulder of his jacket.

The woman fled into the house, upsetting the pail of milk as she left. Stacey wondered whether he should stay or flee, but the decision was quickly made for him when a young man wearing a military-style uniform came out of the farmhouse and walked straight toward him.

———◆———

The man wearing the uniform was not a German soldier. He was a Belgian game warden and was getting ready to search for poachers. He approached Stacey in a friendly manner, patted the word "Canada" on his jacket and quickly ushered Stacey into the farmhouse.

Stacey was at the home of Jean and Victorine Roemans. The game warden was Alexis Zeevaert, the Roemans' son-in-law, who was married to their daughter Josette. Another daughter, Marietta, who was sixteen, also lived at the home.

When Stacey brought out his silk maps, members of the family informed him by pointing that he was in Belgium. He was in De Plank, a hamlet close to the border between Belgium and the Netherlands. He could not communicate well with the family because no one spoke English. They spoke Flemish and understood some French.

Mrs. Roemans prepared a breakfast of eggs, bacon, black bread, and chicory coffee for Stacey. The family also brought a bottle of red wine and poured two glasses for him.

After breakfast, Zeevaert, the game warden, took Stacey upstairs to a bedroom. After removing his shoes, but still wearing his full battle dress, he lay down on a large double bed and fell asleep.

At this point, Marietta, the sixteen-year-old girl, noticed some food was set aside. She asked why. In Flemish, her father replied, "Kind beloof me dat je niets verder verteld, maar wij hebben een Canadese vliegenier boven." He had said, "Child, promise me you won't tell anyone, but we have a Canadian Air Force soldier upstairs."

Any Belgium resident protecting an Allied soldier risked being arrested, imprisoned, tortured, and executed. Jean Roemans, however, had a particular reason to want to make sure his daughter told no one about the Canadian upstairs. The Gestapo, the German secret police, already knew him. Gestapo agents had interrogated Roemans and his family after learning that he was thinking of setting up a radio, which was illegal. Although he hadn't installed a radio, the agents ransacked the farmhouse looking for it. The Gestapo also put him in prison for three weeks, giving him only bread and water.

———◆———

In the evening, Zeevaert knocked on the bedroom door. By then, Stacey was awake. Zeevaert brought him civilian clothes: grey flannel trousers, a shirt, socks, and a beret.

Stacey gave his uniform to the family. "Fumez," he said, using his high school French. He was aware that he and his uniform put the family at risk.

In order to leave as quickly as possible, Stacey wanted the family to help him contact the Resistance movement that was fighting the German forces occupying Belgium. Speaking with Zeevaert and Roemans in their living room, Stacey uttered words he hoped would enable them to understand what he wanted. "Underground," he said. The two men appeared not to understand. "La Resistance," he then said. No response. "Maquis," he said. The two Belgian men appeared to know that word, which was the name of the French Resistance, but they didn't seem to understand what it was he wanted them to do.

At one point, Stacey pulled out a card of phrases in various languages that the air force had given him to use if he were in a foreign country. Flemish wasn't on the card, but French was. Zeevaert and Roemans became agitated when they read a question about the closest border. They were concerned because the closest border was very close. The farmhouse was only 200 metres from the border with the Netherlands. During the war, German guards manned the border post twenty-four hours a day.

Gordon Stacey did not have to wait long before seeing someone from the border station. Early the next morning, Sunday, April 30, he heard a motorcycle screech to a halt outside the house. Stacey looked out of a window and saw a German sergeant get off the motorcycle and walk up to the house. As soon as he saw the sergeant, Stacey scrambled under the bed in his room. After a few minutes, he heard the motorcycle drive away.

Zeevaert found Stacey under the bed and encouraged him to come out. By using pictures and sign language, Zeevaert informed Stacey that the sergeant was not looking for him. A German soldier came to the farmhouse every morning to buy eggs for the guards at the nearby border post. From then on, Stacey stayed in his room until the Germans had their eggs for the day.

Back in Canada the air force informed Stacey's parents that their son was missing in action. Hilda Stacey received her telegram at her home in Toronto. Austin Stacey received his in Hamilton, where he was serving at an army training school. Stacey's mother refused to believe her son had been killed. Stacey's father feared the worst.

After a few days at the Roemans' farmhouse, Gordon Stacey's life started to become routine. He stayed indoors during the day and went out to the back of the property in the evenings.

Even though he didn't know whether the family would help him to contact the Resistance, he decided to accept their hospitality. They appeared to wish him well by shaking his hand and patting him on the shoulder. He wondered if this was how he would spend the rest of the war.

The routine was broken one evening when a man identified only as "Le Comte" — The Count — came to the farmhouse. He spoke broken English, which he had learned in England during the First World War. Le Comte asked several questions. Stacey explained how he arrived at the farmhouse, but he avoided giving any military information in case this person was a German agent posing as a member of the Resistance. Le Comte told Stacey he had friends who would help him, and that he would hear from them within a few days.

Stacey gave Le Comte a small photo of himself that he carried in his emergency kit. The photo was to be used on forged identity papers that he would need if German troops stopped him.

The following Saturday, May 6, Zeevaert told Stacey someone had come to see him. Stacey went to the living room. The visitor was a blond woman in her late thirties.

"Hi there. How've you been?" she said in an English accent as she extended her arm to Stacey. He shook her hand. The woman was a member of the Belgian Resistance. Her code name was Fifi. By extending her arm, she was conducting her first test to determine whether Stacey really was a Canadian Air Force officer or whether he was a German spy. A person raised in continental Europe — such as a German agent — would kiss a woman's hand, not shake it. By shaking Fifi's hand, he had passed the first test.

Fifi then asked Stacey numerous questions, such as the name of a person on a popular British radio program she thought he would have heard at his base in England.

He passed all the tests. For Stacey, this was most fortunate. Fifi had come to the house accompanied by three armed members of the Resistance. They waited outside and were prepared to end the life of someone who was pretending to be an Allied airman in order to infiltrate the Resistance movement.

Fifi gave Stacey a forged identity card containing the photo he had given Le Comte earlier in the week. From now on, he wasn't Gordon Stacey, a Canadian born on April 25, 1922; he was François Bierna, a Belgian citizen born on August 12, 1917. Because Stacey did not know any of the various languages used in Belgium, he was supposed to be a deaf-mute.

Fifi told Stacey she would bring an extra bicycle to the house the next day, and that they would ride to the city of Liege, which was about thirty kilometres away.

Several other people would be in the riding party: the daughter of a friend of Fifi's, another member of the Belgian Resistance, and Zeevaert. Fifi chose a Sunday afternoon because many Belgians went bicycling at that time. This would enable Stacey and his escorts to blend in easily.

She checked Stacey's clothes and beret to make sure they were suitable. She was impressed. "You look more like a Belgian than the Belgians do," she said. Nevertheless, Stacey carried his identification tags to prove he was an Allied officer, just in case German soldiers or Gestapo agents stopped him, realized he wasn't Belgian, and arrested him.

Fifi arrived the next day with the bicycles. She and her friend's daughter would ride about fifty metres ahead. Zeevaert and the man in the Resistance would be fifty metres behind.

She told Stacey that if Germans stopped her, he was to turn around, ride in the opposite direction, and not even acknowledge the two men riding with him. They would follow.

Stacey and his escorts set off after lunch on a warm, sunny day. They meandered through the countryside, following the bank of the Meuse River. As Fifi expected, the roads were crowded with cyclists. At one point, there were so many bicycles that Stacey had trouble seeing the two women who were riding in front of him.

After about two hours, they arrived in Liege. They rode across a bridge that took them over a branch of the Meuse River onto Outremeuse island, the centre of the city. Then they cycled to a pedestrian bridge across the main branch of the river on the other side of the island.

Stacey blended in well with the Belgian cyclists, but as he pushed his bike across the bridge, a man in a black uniform stepped in front of him and blocked his way. Stacey understood the significance of that uniform. Black was the colour of the Gestapo, the German secret police.

"Fumez," said the member of the Gestapo as a cigarette dangled from his mouth. The Gestapo agent was seeking a match, not an evader. Stacey put his hand in his pocket, pulled out a book of matches and lit the cigarette.

Later, Stacey realized he had come close to revealing his identity. The matchbook was from his emergency kit. If the Gestapo agent had examined it closely, he would have seen it had a plain white cover that said nothing about the company that made it. The agent might have guessed that it wasn't a matchbook made in or near Belgium and that Stacey wasn't from Belgium.

Pleased to have his cigarette lit, the Gestapo agent didn't look at the matchbook and let Stacey continue to cross the bridge. Stacey found out later that the Gestapo headquarters in Liege was on the island. The agent was probably either going to or leaving the headquarters.

Stacey and his escorts continued on their trip. The two men rode up to him and indicated that they were departing. They had done their job.

The two women and Stacey soon stopped at a white, four-storey house surrounded by a stone wall. It was at 45 Monulphe Street. This was his new home. Fifi took him into the house where she introduced him to another flyer who had been shot down, Flying Officer Dick Taylor, a member of Britain's Royal Air Force.

Taylor gave Stacey a tour of the house, showing him his bedroom, a sunroom that contained a rowing machine he could use to stay in shape, and the attic, which provided a good view of the neighbourhood.

He warned Stacey to stay away from windows so that no one could see him. When Stacey looked out on Monulphe Street, he could see a building about 200 metres away, whose residents would have been very interested in him. The building was the Jonfosse teacher-training school, but the German army was using it as a base for an engineering unit. Outside the building each morning the German soldiers lined up in four rows for inspection. A sergeant followed the inspecting officer, jotting points in a notebook as they went along.

"If they only knew," Stacey said to himself as he watched the soldiers without getting too close to the windows.

Stacey and Taylor often slept during the day and stayed awake at night because that was the time German agents raided houses looking for Allied flyers. They had to be ready to leave quickly.

Fifi had set up an escape plan for them. She placed a short ladder at the end of the garden, beside the wall. If the Germans raided the house, the men would use the ladder to climb over the wall. They would hide in the bushes on the other side. The last one over would pull the ladder to the other side. She also gave them small pistols that she was able to obtain because her father was a gun manufacturer.

That was the entire plan. Fifi might call them back or she might be unable to do so. The Germans could have arrested her. If that happened, they could be on their own again — an unpleasant fate, but preferable to Fifi's.

At this point in the war, Allied aircraft often dropped bombs in the Liege area. Air raid sirens wailed constantly. When Stacey heard the siren, he didn't go to a shelter; he went to the attic to watch the bombardment. The Allied bombers were aiming at targets in the industrial east side of the city. On a map provided by a member of the Resistance, Stacey plotted where he thought the bombs had fallen. Later, members of the Resistance confirmed that his calculations were quite accurate. Stacey also watched Allied and German fighter pilots battle one another. The fighting was fierce. Planes from both sides were shot down. Sometimes the pilots bailed out; sometimes they didn't.

With the increasing number of Allied flights in the area, there were more downed flyers. Fifi moved Taylor to another safe house and brought two American flyers, Staff Sergeant Harold Booth and Lieutenant Joel Punches, to 45 Monulphe Street.

Stacey knew the air battles were a prelude to the Allied invasion. The ill-fated flight of LL243 had been part of the campaign leading to the invasion. The day was getting closer when Allied troops would start pushing German soldiers back to their own country, liberating France, Belgium, and the Netherlands.

———◆———

In quieter moments, when not helping the Resistance or worrying about German raids, Fifi, a lively woman, would think back to the pre-war years. She kept the memory of that era alive partly by playing a record of Maurice Chevalier's signature song "Louise" on her gramophone. Fifi had seen the French entertainer at a concert in Belgium. She apparently caught his eye, and when he sang that song, he substituted her name for Louise.

She was also keenly interested in the English spoken by the different airmen who stayed with her. She noted not just the various accents of flyers from Britain, Canada, and the United States, but also the different rhythms which they used when speaking.

To help Stacey pass the time, Fifi managed to obtain a model of a Halifax bomber for him to build. This was the aircraft he had flown on his last flight. Stacey had no idea how she found a model of a British war plane in a country occupied by German forces.

———◆———

The day that Stacey had been waiting for came on June 6, 1944, five-and-a-half weeks after LL243 was shot down.

"They've landed. They've landed," Jeanne Delwaide, a member of the Resistance, said when she came to the house that day. A woman in her sixties, Delwaide had a fierce hatred of Germany that went back to the First World War, when German troops overran her country for the first time.

Stacey and others in the house turned on their radio to listen to the British Broadcasting Corporation. Yes, the Allies had landed. This was D-Day. British, American, and Canadian troops were on the beaches of Normandy.

Later that day, General Dwight Eisenhower, the Supreme Allied Commander, addressed Western Europeans in a radio broadcast. Eisenhower urged members of Resistance movements to show restraint and patience. He did not want them to stage premature uprisings.

Stacey listened to Eisenhower's speech with mixed feelings. Though delighted that the Allies were in France, he knew he could not expect to be liberated quickly. He had to be patient.

Nazi Germany still occupied Belgium and it was still powerful. One day, Fifi feared the Germans were about to raid the house. She took the flyers staying there to separate homes. While walking to another house about a kilometre away, she and Stacey saw a German soldier with a rifle standing at the entrance to a train tunnel.

"Take it easy," Fifi said. Stacey was nervous, but he trusted her. He took it easy. Acting nonchalantly, he walked by the German soldier. The guard did not stop him. Stacey stayed at the other house for the night, but returned to Monulphe Street the next day.

———◆———

Several months after LL243 crashed, Stacey's father, Austin, learned by reading casualty reports that four members of his son's crew had been killed and that one was a prisoner of war. He read nothing about his son. While at Fifi's house, Stacey had no means of telling his parents what had happened to him.

Hilda continued to believe her son was alive. Her faith was so strong that she did not tell anyone he was safe. She feared German authorities would start searching for him if they knew he was alive. She wanted them to leave him alone.

———————◆———————

After D-Day, Stacey plotted the progress of the Allied troops in Normandy, and then in other parts of France and Belgium. Week by week, as spring turned into summer, the American army moved closer to Liege.

By early September he could hear artillery barrages and machine guns in the distance. The German troops, including many who were wounded, were retreating. The soldiers in the engineering unit in the school on Monulphe Street left as quickly as they could.

"You don't have to go out yet," Fifi told Stacey. "You stay where you are. I'll let you know when you can go out."

Then, on September 8, General Omar Bradley's First U.S. Army arrived in Liege and set up camp at the Park of the Boverie, on Outremeuse island.

Fifi, however, was still cautious. She didn't want to go out of her house with all three airmen at one time. A group of four people could be a target for lone snipers who were still in the city. The two Americans, Booth and Punches, would walk together, and she and Stacey would do the same.

With Stacey, Fifi strolled to the park to meet the American troops. On their way, they saw women with shaved heads walking on the streets. Members of the Resistance had identified them as having helped the Germans and had marked them by cutting off their hair. The Resistance was taking them to prison.

At the park, about thirty-five American soldiers had set up camp. Fifi approached a sergeant standing beside an armoured vehicle. "Is there anything we can get you?" she asked.

"We'd love a shower," the sergeant said. The American soldiers had been travelling for several days with few chances to stop. Fifi said she would contact a public swimming pool that had showers. A lieutenant then approached and asked Stacey who he was and what he was doing.

Stacey identified himself as a Canadian Air Force officer. The lieutenant told him to go to the city hall in a few days. By then, the Americans would have placed an administrator in charge of the city. The administrator would help him to leave Liege.

This was a joyful day in Liege. The city's residents swarmed into the park to celebrate. Belgian flags, Union Jacks, and flags of other Allied countries flew from windows throughout the city.

In the evening, one of Fifi's neighbours invited Stacey to a celebration. The neighbours said they suspected Fifi and the Resistance were hiding Allied servicemen. They drew this conclusion from the number of people going into the house. Wine flowed freely during the evening and into the early hours of the next day. For the residents of Liege, the war was over. Stacey, who had been hiding from Germans for more than four months, also believed his participation in the war was over. However, he would soon find out that he was wrong.

———————◆———————

A few days later, Stacey went to the city hall to meet a colonel whom the American army had appointed as the city's administrator. Stacey asked the colonel to notify his parents in Canada and an uncle in England that he was alive and well. He also asked the colonel if he would approve travel passes permitting him and Fifi to return to the farmhouse at De Plank. He wanted to thank the Roemans for helping him.

The colonel checked a huge map on a wall in his office, and he saw that the Americans had pushed the German army out of the part of Belgium where the farmhouse was located. He gave Stacey the passes.

Stacey and Fifi bicycled back to the farmhouse on a warm, sunny day with just a few clouds. The Roemans were thrilled to see him. They presented him with a large box tied with string. The box contained his uniform — the one he had given to the family, along with the one-word instruction in French: "Fumez!" Instead of burning the uniform, the family had cleaned and pressed it.

Stacey knew they had saved his uniform to honour him, but he was astounded that they had kept something for five months that could have provided indisputable evidence that they had helped an Allied officer.

The uniform upset Fifi. She knew that if German agents had found it, the family would have been interrogated and could have revealed information about Stacey, herself, and the Resistance.

Later that afternoon, Stacey went into the farmyard to show Fifi where he met Victorine Roemans when she was milking the goats. While they were in the yard, two fighter planes roared overhead at about 600 metres. An American Thunderbolt was chasing a German Messerschmitt. A puff of smoke emerged from the Thunderbolt. It had fired on the German plane. Pieces of the Messerschmitt then broke away from it, and the plane flipped over. The pilot bailed out, opening his parachute moments before he reached the ground.

Many of the residents of the hamlet went outside when they heard the planes. As soon as the German pilot bailed out, some went back to their homes to get weapons such as pitchforks.

The tall, blond, blue-eyed pilot landed in a nearby field. The residents approached him.

He put his hands above his head. "Kamerad," said the frightened pilot, trying to be friendly by using the German word for comrade. He was only a teenager.

The residents searched his pockets, removing his Luger pistol and his maps. Fifi was concerned that they would harm him, but Stacey was reluctant to become involved. He had more experience evading Germans than guarding them.

"You better get over there," Fifi said, reminding him that he was an Allied officer. Fifi and Stacey then approached the pilot. She took control of the crowd and the pilot's pistol. She then declared that Stacey was in charge and handed the pistol to him.

An older resident who spoke German assured the pilot that he would be properly treated. Stacey intended to take the pilot to the farmhouse, but as they walked toward it, an American jeep with a driver and a lieutenant pulled up beside them. Stacey explained to them what had happened, and gave the pistol to the lieutenant.

Fifi and Stacey watched as the jeep drove away. The German pilot sat in the passenger seat; the American lieutenant was behind him, watching him closely. For Flying Officer Gordon Stacey, the war against Nazi Germany was finally over.

———————◆———————

Having visited the Roemans, Stacey's goal was to return to England. This was not easy because the Allied troops were moving eastward toward Germany. He wanted to go west.

The British army's headquarters on continental Europe was in Brussels, so Stacey decided to go there. Booth and Punches, the two Americans, wanted to go to Paris where the U.S. Army had set up its headquarters.

Fifi arranged for a Red Cross car to take them to Brussels, but it didn't have gasoline for the trip. Booth and Punches solved the problem by visiting an American army unit that had moved into the teachers college on Monulphe Street, after the German army vacated it. The unit provided two cans of gasoline.

The three airmen and Fifi set off for Brussels at the end of summer, on September 21. Booth and Punches went on to Paris that day. Stacey stayed overnight at the headquarters. The next day, he got into a truck that took him to an airport for a flight on a Dakota transport plane to London. Fifi went to the airport to see him leave.

His departure was emotionally wrenching. Fifi had risked her life to help him. He made sure he had her real name, knowing that he would try to contact her after the war ended.

———————◆———————

Fifi was really Mabel Fraipont. "Fifi" was her nickname, which she used as a code name. When not helping the Allies, Fifi — or, rather, Mabel Fraipont — worked as a seamstress, sewing curtains and dresses at her country home, not far from the Roemans' farmhouse. She was a single woman.

Her mother, Constance, was born in England, which explained her fluency in English. Her father, Emile, was a Belgian citizen. Fraipont had helped the British army as it retreated from Dunkirk, France, in the spring of 1940. While holidaying near Ostend, a Belgian city on the North Sea not far from Dunkirk, she came across British troops hiding from the Germans, who had occupied Belgium and part of France. She brought the soldiers food and quietly arranged for boats to take them back to Britain.

A friend of the Fraiponts working with the Belgian Resistance soon approached the family to ask if they could provide a room at their house where members of the Allied forces could hide while evading the Germans. Fraipont's father agreed.

She soon learned how dangerous this could be. A former boyfriend of her younger sister, Lucie, informed the German authorities that an Allied flyer, Sergeant Harry Fraser, was at their

Mabel Vraipont.

house. The Germans arrested Emile and Constance Fraipont, as well as Lucie. Fraipont's parents were supposed to be executed, but Hermann Goering, the highest ranking member of the German military, wasn't available to sign the execution papers. As a result, they were sent to concentration camps in Germany. Her father went to Buchenwald, which was near Weimar, and her mother went to Dachau, near Munich. Lucie was also incarcerated. German authorities did not think Mabel Fraipont was involved. She decided to continue using her parents' home as a safe house because she doubted the Germans would suspect the Resistance would use a house after they had raided it.

After leaving Brussels, the Dakota carrying Stacey couldn't fly straight for London. It had to take a southerly route over France to avoid flying over the Netherlands, where Germany and the Allies were still fighting. When flying at a low level over the Falaise area of France, the airmen could literally smell the war. This was a battleground that the German army had only recently vacated, leaving thousands of dead soldiers on the ground. Their decomposing bodies created a stench noticeable from the air.

Soon, however, Stacey could see a more pleasant scene: the white cliffs of Dover. At that point, he knew he was just minutes away from arriving in England. The Dakota landed at Northolt airbase near London. When Stacey and the other airmen left the plane, armed guards were waiting for them. The guards were responsible for escorting all the men by truck to an office where MI9, the British intelligence service, interrogated them. Intelligence officers wanted to know about their experiences as evaders, and who had helped them.

The officer who interviewed Stacey had files on Stacey's crew and told him that two members of his crew were alive and four had died. He informed Stacey that Johnny Arscott, the bomb-aimer who was helped by the Dutch Resistance, had just returned to England, and Alan Fuller, the flight engineer who police arrested in a Dutch house, was a prisoner of war. He also said that the four members of the crew who died were buried at the Maastricht General Cemetery in the Netherlands.

The intelligence officer ordered Stacey not to reveal what he knew to anyone. German forces were still fighting fiercely, and the Allies did not want information about the Resistance to be publicly disclosed.

Stacey then phoned his uncle, Alec Pierson, who lived with his wife, Hilda, in Surrey, near London. His aunt answered the phone. "It's Gordon," Stacey said. He heard the phone drop. After several minutes, his uncle picked up the telephone receiver and explained that he had had to take care of his wife. She had passed out when she heard her nephew's voice. Although his aunt knew he was alive, she had not known he was back in England. After enduring years of warfare, the shock of hearing his voice had overpowered her.

Stacey's uncle arranged for him to visit them later that day.

After another few weeks in England, Stacey boarded the *Queen Elizabeth* ocean liner at Liverpool, which took him to Boston. From there he took a train to Ottawa, and then an overnight train to Toronto.

After the train arrived at Union Station on Sunday, November 5, he took a streetcar to his parents' home at 16 Ardrossan Place. His family hugged and kissed him. Stacey's father, who earlier in the year had feared his son was dead, was in tears. His mother was less emotional because she never doubted he was alive.

Stacey arrived early enough to go with his family to Bedford Park United Church for the weekly service. Reverend George Wood, the minister, had not seen Stacey arrive at the church, but he informed the congregation that Stacey was safely back in England.

"He's here," a member of the congregation said. Indeed he was.

After the service, everyone wanted to know what had happened, but following the order of the intelligence officer, he did not reveal any details.

His parents were relieved that he was home, but the war against Germany was far from over. Furthermore, Stacey had volunteered to participate in the war against Japan in the Pacific.

In December, the German army launched a counteroffensive through the Ardennes forest in southeast Belgium, to regain territory it had lost. This offensive became known as the Battle of the Bulge. Stacey feared German troops would again control the area around Liege. He knew that if this happened, the Germans would try to arrest Fraipont because, by this time, her work with the Resistance was well known. By mid-January 1945, the Allies stopped the German advance before it got to Liege. Only then did Stacey feel that Fraipont was safe.

Near the end of the war, on April 6, 1945, the Germans forced Alan Fuller, the flight engineer, and other prisoners at the camp at Fallingbostel, in northwest Germany, to move away from the advancing British troops. After walking through farmland in a northeast direction for three days, he and two other prisoners escaped. They soon came across a casualty centre that the British army had set up as it moved deeper into Germany. Fuller then returned to England.

Although Stacey was willing to fight against Japan, the air force decided it no longer needed his services. It demobilized him in April 1945, a month before the war against Germany ended, and several months before two atomic bombs ended the war against Japan.

Stacey stayed in Toronto where he entered an electrical engineering program at the University of Toronto.

In 1947, two years after the war ended, Stacey returned to Belgium where he met Mabel Fraipont again. All members of her family survived the war, but her parents died within a few years. The harsh life in the concentration camps broke their spirits and damaged their health.

In a report she wrote in 1947, Fraipont revealed that in addition to protecting Allied airmen, she attended a dinner party for high ranking German officers supposedly to thank them for their services. She used this opportunity to learn about German operations in the Liege area. Through the officers, she secretly obtained official seals used to authenticate documents. She presented the seals to the Belgian Resistance, which copied them, and she returned them without being caught.

Fraipont also said in that report she had not received any money from the Allies to feed and clothe the flyers who stayed with her. She covered the costs by selling her jewellery and other personal items.

After graduating from university, Stacey moved to Guelph, Ontario, where he joined the Guelph Board of Light and Heat Commissioners, which later became Guelph Hydro. He spent twenty-five years as the utility's general manager.

He joined the Royal Air Forces Escaping Society, which was set up after the war to honour the men and women who had helped airmen while they were evading German forces. He was also a founding member of the Canadian branch of the society, which was formed just before Canada's centennial year, 1967. He later served a term as president of the branch.

For a centennial year project in 1967, the Canadian branch decided to invite members of Resistance movements from several countries to Canada. The society accepted Stacey's suggestion that it invite Mabel Fraipont. While in Ottawa, Fraipont and other members of the group visited the House of Commons. The parliamentarians greeted them with an enthusiastic applause. She also met the prime minister, Lester Pearson, at a reception given to honour them.

Fraipont died in 1992.

With the inevitable aging of its members, and those they helped, the Canadian branch of the evaders society decided to cease operating as an official organization in 2005. Its members, however, still get together socially.

Stacey has returned to Europe several times since the war. In 1994, he went to commemorate the fiftieth anniversary of LL243 being shot down. The council near Gulpen in the Netherlands erected a stone memorial to honour Stacey's crewmates. Children attending a nearby school will look after the monument. The other two surviving members of the crew, Alan Fuller and Johnny Arscott, also attended.

While on that trip, Stacey picked up a fact sheet written by a Dutch resident, Ron Putz, identifying the pilot who shot down LL243 as First Lieutenant Georg Fengler.

Caroline McLachlan Darling

Gordon Stacey in 2006.

Marietta Roemans, the sixteen-year-old girl whom Stacey met at the farmhouse, will be eighty-two in 2010. She still lives in the house, along with her husband, Josef Beuken. They no longer use the property as a farm. Their son, Bruno, now uses part of the house to run a trucking company.

Marietta remembers the days that Stacey stayed at her home during the war as a time of fear. She was worried that if the Germans discovered him, they would shoot members of her family.

Gordon Stacey, who will be eighty-eight in 2010, still marvels at Mabel Fraipont's courage, stamina, and dedication. Talking about her as he sat on an outdoor patio at his home in Guelph, Stacey said she didn't discuss the danger she was in. Instead, she talked about the danger he was in.

Stacey still has mementoes from his last flight on LL243, including the metal ring from the end of the ripcord, a package of Horlick's tablets, the maps he opened at the Roemans' farmhouse, the matchbook he used when he lit the Gestapo agent's cigarette, and the uniform that the Roemans kept for him. But what he most treasures is the memory of an amazing woman who risked her life to save him and other Allied flyers.

12
THE ESCORT

In 1941, Dick Watson wanted to put on a uniform, but he wasn't thinking of a military one. Watson, an eighteen-year-old resident of Oba in northern Ontario, wanted to be a Mountie and wear a red tunic. The Mounties who visited Oba impressed him.

Watson went to Ottawa to join the police force. The RCMP accepted him, but he didn't like a comment that a senior RCMP officer made to him and other applicants. The officer told them they shouldn't join the force as a way of avoiding military service. He said the RCMP might send them to Europe to direct traffic.

Watson felt insulted. The officer was implying that he was afraid of military service. He wasn't afraid to serve in the military; he wanted to be a Mountie.

Dick Watson

Dick Watson in Toronto in 1942.

He walked out of the building, which was near the National War Memorial, and saw a recruiting booth for the Royal Canadian Air Force. He walked to it and asked if he could enlist.

He impressed the officers in the booth. Watson had all of his application documents with him — the same documents he had just shown the RCMP. The air force accepted him immediately.

The next day Watson was at the RCAF depot on the grounds of the Canadian National Exhibition in Toronto. The Royal Canadian Air Force was ready to train Watson to be a pilot.

———————◆———————

Three years later, in the spring of 1944, Warrant Officer Dick Watson flew from England to targets in France. After the invasion of Normandy on June 6, 1944, he moved to a base at Bayeux, France. He was serving with the RCAF's 440 Squadron.

On July 18, Watson revved the engine of his Typhoon fighter-bomber to get ready for another bombing flight. Watson and seven other Typhoon pilots from his squadron were going to attack a German mortar position a few kilometres southeast of Caen, a city in Normandy. The mortar guns had been firing at Allied soldiers.

The squadron's attack was part of Operation Goodwood, a campaign to push German troops away from Caen. British soldiers, along with Polish troops, were ready to move into the area.

Watson took off for the mortar guns just after the sun rose. His Typhoon, like the other Typhoons, carried two thousand-pound bombs. The sky was clear, unlike the cloudy skies immediately after the invasion that had hindered Allied planes. As he flew, a British artillery unit fired shells at the mortar guns to mark the target. The shells released purple smoke that the Typhoon pilots could easily see.

After flying for fifteen minutes, Watson started diving straight down, toward the mortar guns at about 640 kilometres an hour. Then he released the two bombs.

Within seconds, something hit Watson's plane. He presumed it was a German artillery shell. His Typhoon exploded. The wings fell off.

Watson had to get out of the aircraft immediately. He knew exactly what to do — he had often practised the ejection procedure while sitting in a Typhoon cockpit back at his base: First, release the safety harness that kept a pilot strapped in the aircraft.

Second, pull the red lever on the right side of the cockpit windshield to jettison the canopy.

Third, push the control column forward to eject the pilot from the cockpit.

Watson followed the procedure. As soon as he was out of the aircraft he felt the air rush by his face. The force of the wind also ripped away all the loose items he carried, such as his pistol. In a state of shock, Watson did not realize he had pulled his ripcord until he looked up and saw his parachute.

As Watson descended, a German soldier in the target area fired a machine gun at him. About one hundred bullets went through his parachute, but it still functioned. One bullet took the heel off his right shoe. Another went through his Mae West life jacket, just missing him.

Watson knew that the soldier was aiming at him because he saw the red glow of tracer bullets coming from the machine gun. He pulled the risers, or parachute cords, to move as far from the gunner as he could, but the gunner kept firing, even after he landed in a wheat field about 200 metres away.

Watson lay flat in a furrow. The wheat was about a metre high, and he could hear the bullets hitting the grain, just over his head.

He didn't panic. As a northern Ontario boy, Watson felt prepared to deal with whatever problems confronted him. The only thought he had in his mind was survival.

The German gunner eventually ceased firing, but Watson soon had another problem. The British army started firing artillery shells at the German troops who were near him. Some shells landed so close that the sandy soil thrown into the air by the explosions landed on him.

Shortly after the artillery barrage, heavy Allied bombers flew over the target. They dropped what seemed like a cloud of bombs. The ground shook.

Then Watson saw a German tank coming directly toward him through the wheat. When the tank was about ten metres away, he rolled to get out of its path. The tank driver wasn't looking for him or other Allied servicemen — he was retreating.

***

At about noon, when he was no longer worried about a German gunner firing at him or Allied bombs and shells hitting him, Watson raised his head. He could see about fifty tanks a kilometre away. These were British tanks, and they were ready to advance through the French countryside.

Soon, one of the tanks came into the wheat field. Watson approached it. The tank commander who was standing in the hatch recognized him. "Dick Watson, what are you doing here?" he asked.

Watson was surprised that anyone in the tank knew him, but when it got closer he recognized the commander as Major Theron. Watson had flown the major when he watched tank manoeuvres during exercises in England. The pilot explained to Theron that he had been shot down. Theron, a forward tank observer, reported to artillery and tank units following behind. While Watson and Theron talked, five German soldiers ran toward them.

***

Back in London, Foreign Secretary Anthony Eden spoke to the House of Commons about the war. Eden said that the Allies had prepared peace terms to offer Germany, even though he did not want to discuss them publicly. "Victory cannot come too quick," he said.

———◆———

For the German soldiers running toward the tank, the war could not come to an end quickly enough. The soldiers had their hands above their heads, and they discarded their weapons. The Germans did not want to attack Watson and Theron, but to surrender to them. The soldiers had seen the power of the Allies that morning. They didn't want to fight the tanks that were coming toward them because they didn't want to die.

Theron couldn't stop to look after the prisoners. He had to help the army move forward. He suggested that Watson escort them to the British lines by following the tracks that the tank had made through the wheat fields.

Before Theron moved on, a British soldier walking with the tank used his knife to cut a piece of Watson's parachute. He gave it to Watson to keep as a memento.

The German prisoners were young men, about Watson's age. One of the soldiers talked to Watson in broken English. The soldier showed him a photo of his wife and little girls.

Watson and the prisoners started walking along the path made by the tank. He was limping because he had hurt his right knee when he ejected from his Typhoon.

Although Watson was not armed, he did not feel threatened by the prisoners. He was pleased to have them around him because he thought they provided him with a form of protection. By staying in the middle of the group, he hoped German snipers in the area would not fire at him.

At first, the prisoners held their hands above their heads, but as they walked along they became more casual. Other German soldiers saw the group and decided to surrender. They came out of their foxholes a hundred metres away and joined the line. Before long, Watson was escorting twenty-five prisoners, then fifty, then a hundred, and, finally, about 120.

The German prisoners were congenial. Not one showed anger or hostility to him or the Allies. They just walked quietly.

The prisoners' march came to an end when Watson arrived at a British first aid station. At the station, the 120 prisoners lay on the ground.

Watson helped look after some of the wounded Allied soldiers. A lot of the soldiers were Polish troops fighting with a British armoured unit. Many suffered burns when German eighty-eight-millimetre shells hit their tanks, setting them on fire. Watson applied a purple gel to their burns.

After being at the first aid station for about two hours, Watson and the prisoners departed for a fenced compound a few kilometres away. The army used a Bren gun carrier to lead the prisoners to the compound. Watson rode on the carrier along with a wounded German soldier. The other Germans walked behind. As Watson and the prisoners moved toward the compound, they passed Allied infantry troops on their way to attack the Germans.

The prisoners arrived at the compound in the late afternoon. Watson approached a sergeant and explained what had happened.

"Do you want a receipt for the prisoners?" the sergeant asked.

"What the heck do I want that for?" Watson replied. He was happy just to leave the prisoners there.

The army then drove Watson to a nearby airfield so he could be flown back to his base.

At the airfield, he met a boyhood friend, Flying Officer Bill Bliss of Toronto. Bliss, a Spitfire pilot, told the communications department at the airfield what had happened to Watson that day. The department was intrigued and took a photo of the two flyers holding a piece of Watson's parachute.

Watson then flew back to his base at Bayeux, arriving at about 7:00 p.m. Dr. Roger Dunn, 440 Squadron's medical officer, gave Watson a quick examination and concluded that he needed nothing but two Aspirin. The squadron, however, gave Watson a more appealing prescription: two weeks leave in London.

After enjoying London's night life, Watson returned to his base and resumed his regular duties. He went on numerous bombing and strafing flights. The squadron was constantly on standby. It could be airborne in five minutes and over a target in another ten.

On January 1, 1945, when 440 Squadron was based at Eindhoven in the Netherlands, Watson was on a taxiing runway, getting ready to take off on a reconnaissance flight.

The Luftwaffe had chosen that day to launch a campaign known as Operation Bodenplatte — Operation Ground Plate.

Watson could see German fighter planes flying toward the base. He decided to use his plane like a cannon. He moved his Typhoon off the runway onto the frozen grass, and angled it so that he could fire at the German fighters flying above the runway. He opened the throttle just enough to raise the nose so he could aim at the fighters.

He fired his twenty-millimetre cannons at the two German F190s. Watson knew he had hit one because pieces of the aircraft flew off it.

The German planes fired at his Typhoon. Watson's fuel tank exploded. He had to jump out. His eyebrows were singed by the fire, but otherwise he was not injured. As he jumped, however, he reinjured his right knee, which swelled up. The entire plane burned.

Immediately after the Eindhoven raid, Watson flew back to England where he spent two weeks in hospital. His right eye had become infected, possibly by a particle that had entered it when he ejected from his Typhoon.

After the hospital released him, Watson became an instructor at RAF Millfield in Northumberland, in northern England. He returned to Canada after the war, on the ocean liner *Cape Town Castle*.

In September 1945, the RCMP asked Watson if he would like to join the force. It had kept his application on file since 1941. The Mounties offered him seniority going back to the day he had enlisted in the RCAF. By this time, however, Watson did not want to wear the uniform of either the Mounties or the air force. He wanted to wear the uniform of a fishing guide.

Ian Darling

Dick Watson in 2008.

Watson bought a small tourist camp where he had worked as a teenager. He built up the business and turned it into a lodge. Watson, who will be eighty-seven in 2010, now lives in a long-term care centre in Sault Ste. Marie, Ontario. His family still operates the tourist business.

Dick Watson acknowledges that he made one mistake the day he was shot down. He regrets that he didn't accept a receipt for the prisoners he escorted. The receipt would have been a wonderful memento of an incredible day.

13
FLYING LESSONS

Flying Officer Ralph Campbell was feeling rather confident on August 27, 1944. The previous day he had successfully flown his Stirling bomber through a violent thunderstorm in France. Campbell, the pilot, was particularly pleased because he and his crew managed to return to their base in England on three engines. The fourth wasn't working. The members of his crew congratulated one another — they thought they could overcome just about any problem.

Campbell was twenty-five, a farm boy from Foxboro in eastern Ontario. He was flying with the Royal Air Force's 196 Squadron, based at Keevil, near Bristol, England. With him were three other Canadians, Flying Officer Art Capes, the bomb-aimer, from Saskatchewan; Flying Officer Ed Leadlay, the navigator, from Guelph; and Flight Sergeant

Ralph Campbell

Ralph Campbell's crew: (from top left) Ted Dodds, Ralph Campbell, Ed Leadlay, and Pete Boddington; (from bottom left) Sid McQuillan and Frank Gladwin. Not all the airmen in the photo were in both flights mentioned in this chapter.

Frank Gladwin, the rear gunner, from Ottawa. The other two were English: Sergeant Sid McQuillan, the wireless operator, from Yorkshire, and Sergeant Ted Dodds, the flight engineer, from Durham.

In the evening, Campbell and his crew took off again for France. Their goal was to drop supplies to the French Resistance in central France. They were in a different Stirling because the one they had used the previous night had to be repaired. The plane's call letters were EF311, but it was known around the base as "I for Item."

As I for Item approached the French coast, the inner engine on the port side burst into flames. Campbell pushed a button to activate the fire extinguisher. The fire went out, but the propeller no longer worked properly. It turned, but didn't have the power to turn quickly enough to pull the aircraft.

Campbell wondered what his crew thought. "Anybody think we should turn back?" he asked on the intercom. He suspected his crew would tell him to continue. He was right. They told him to carry on.

Campbell continued, but he wanted to feather the propeller on the malfunctioning engine. This would turn the blades inward and keep them motionless, thereby reducing the drag on the aircraft and enabling Campbell to fly on three engines, just as he did the night before.

He pushed the feathering lever, but the propeller continued to turn slowly. He alerted Dodds, the flight engineer. Dodds said there was no other way to solve the problem. "We'll just have to let it revolve." Campbell flew on.

When the aircraft was close to its destination, Campbell looked for, and saw, a Morse code signal sent by a member of the Resistance holding a flashlight. The signal confirmed that the aircraft was in the right area. The crew dropped twenty-four containers and three packages then headed home. Everything appeared to be fine. Campbell felt confident.

Suddenly, while over the English Channel at about 7,000 feet (2,100 metres), the port inner engine made a deafening whine. The plane started vibrating. Campbell looked at his tachometer, which showed whether the engine was racing. It was. The propeller was turning so quickly it could easily have flown off the plane.

"Ralph, are you all right?" said Leadlay, the navigator. Leadlay was shouting but Campbell could only just hear him. "I'm OK," he said.

Normally, the crew referred to Campbell as "Skipper" when they were in the air and "Ralph" when on the ground. Leadlay's use of the pilot's first name showed he feared something was seriously wrong.

Campbell, who was desperately trying to hold the control column, knew I for Item was in trouble. He knew that the propeller's blades could become loose, fly off the plane, and strike it, causing massive damage.

He didn't have to wait long. He heard an explosion, and he felt the aircraft shake. Then he heard silence, and the vibrations ceased. The troublesome propeller had come off the plane and struck the outer port propeller, knocking it off the plane too. I for Item had no engines on its port side.

With two engines on one side not functioning, I for Item couldn't stay in the air for long.

"Ditching procedure," Campbell said on the intercom.

The crew knew what that meant. The plane would soon be in the English Channel. They also knew what to do. Dodds, the flight engineer, emptied the fuel tanks on the port side to make the plane lighter. McQuillan, the wireless operator, sent out SOS messages and opened the astrodome on top of the fuselage — the astrodome is the escape hatch for the central part of the aircraft. The crew also put on their inflatable life jackets, which servicemen called "Mae Wests," a nickname derived from the curvaceous American actress.

Without the port engines to balance the starboard engines, I for Item veered to the port side. Capes, the bomb-aimer, tried to help Campbell stop the plane from turning. As Campbell used his right foot on the pedal that controlled the plane's rudder, Capes applied pressure with his left foot. While Campbell flew the plane, Capes tightened the pilot's safety harness and opened the escape hatch above the cockpit.

I for Item rapidly lost altitude. It was going down at about 500 feet (150 metres) a minute.

Campbell used his radio transmitter. "Mayday! Mayday!" he said, giving the aircraft's location as about twenty-four kilometres south of the Selsey Bill, a small peninsula in West Sussex that juts into the English Channel. He knew the plane could stay in the air for only about ten to twelve minutes from the time it lost its second propeller.

A woman at an airbase somewhere in southern England heard the message. "Stand by, I Item" she said, but Campbell never heard from her again.

His mind crossed the Atlantic and went to his farm in Ontario. He thought of his parents, Fred and Pearl Campbell, and he thought of his friends. Campbell quickly refocused his attention on the aircraft. Because of the dark, cloudy night, he couldn't see the surface of the Channel. He checked his altimeter, which showed the plane's height. "Fifty feet, brace yourselves," Campbell said to his crew.

I for Item hit the water at 2:10 a.m. The plane stopped quickly and the impact threw Campbell forward, but he was not hurt. Water flooded into the cockpit, rising above Campbell's head. He tried to release the pin that held him in his safety harness — the harness that Capes had tightened. Campbell couldn't get the pin out, which meant he couldn't get out of the plane.

———————◆———————

I for Item had gone into the Channel not far from the Nab Tower, which was a few kilometres off the eastern side of the Isle of Wight. The tower was part of an anti-submarine system that Britain built during the First World War. A sentry on the tower saw the plane go down and alerted Air-Sea Rescue.

Within minutes, a launch started searching for I for Item. Later, a second launch joined the search. Two Spitfires were also called upon to look for the aircraft. Neither the crews in the launches, nor the Spitfire pilots, saw any sign of I for Item.

———————◆———————

Campbell tried again to release the pin keeping him in his harness. This time he succeeded. He stood up and climbed out of the escape hatch above him, then swam back to the port wing and climbed onto it. McQuillan was already there. The initial rush of water into the plane had swept him through the astrodome, which he had opened earlier, and onto the fuselage. McQuillan told Campbell that the rubber dinghy the plane carried was inflated and ready for them to enter. The two men scrambled into it.

Soon, the other four members of the crew went through the central escape hatch onto the fuselage and then got into the dinghy. Everyone was alive; everyone was out.

With their hands, the crew paddled the dinghy away from the aircraft so it would not be sucked down when the plane sank. After floating for about ten minutes, I for Item disappeared.

"Is anyone injured in any way?" Campbell asked. Gladwin, the rear gunner, said he couldn't see. A ladder at an escape hatch had come loose and hit him, cutting him near his eye.

Campbell looked at Gladwin's eye. He thought that clotted blood was impairing Gladwin's vision, but that his eye was not injured.

Dodds felt ill. "Just let me slip over the side," he said. He thought he had swallowed fuel. Campbell overruled his flight engineer and kept him inside the dinghy. Campbell and McQuillan rubbed Dodds' back, arms and legs in an attempt to maintain circulation.

The water was rough, and waves crashed against the dinghy, spraying the crew. Fortunately, the Channel was not too cold.

The crew had no compass and the cloudy sky prevented them from using the stars to orient themselves and start going northward, toward England.

The airmen maintained their spirits by singing Frank Sinatra's song, "A Lovely Way to Spend an Evening." After a few hours in the dinghy, they saw the sun rising in the east. Now that the crew had their bearings they used a sheet of rubber that was in the dinghy as a sail, and set off for England.

The crewmates started to feel better. Capes, the bomb-aimer, even started talking about having a warm British beer.

At about 7:00 a.m., the crew saw a small fishing boat in the distance. Two men were in it. The crew shouted and waved. The men in the boat did not respond. Leadlay suspected that the men feared the dinghy contained Germans who would use their fishing boat to take them to France.

Campbell and his crew thought they had to prove from a distance that they were Allied airmen. Leadlay had an idea. He suggested that Dodds shout out to them so that they could hear his northern English accent. Dodds then suggested that the other English airman, McQuillan, call out a list of players with a well-known English football team, Aston Villa. He thought the men in the boat would realize that Germans would not know such information. McQuillan and Dodds called out the appropriate information. The two fishermen then brought their boat close enough to the dinghy to see that the crew were wearing Allied uniforms.

The fishermen were brothers, John and James Lawrence. They said they would take the crew to Selsey, a town on Selsey Bill. The six airmen climbed into the Lawrences' twelve-foot boat. With eight men, the fishing boat was overloaded. After five minutes, it ran out of fuel. The fishermen took out their oars and starting rowing. Because so many men were in the boat, the fishermen could not row properly. One brother used his oar like a paddle; the other used his like a rudder.

The crew was particularly fortunate that the brothers were fishing that night. They had almost decided not to go out because they feared the Channel would be too rough.

The Lawrences told the airmen they had been sailing toward a heavily mined part of the Channel. The British had put the mines along the shoreline earlier in the war to stop German troops from invading.

Campbell and his crew realized that, despite their problems, they were lucky. The defective propeller had not hit the aircraft's fuselage. Their plane had ditched relatively close to England. I for Item remained on the surface long enough for the crew to get out, and the dinghy was inflated. The Lawrences had rescued them and kept them away from the mines.

The fishing boat arrived at Selsey at about 8:30 a.m. The town's residents came to see the airmen, treating them like heroes. The residents took the crew to their community centre and placed them before a warm fire. When they asked if they could get anything for the crew, Capes asked for something he thought about while in the dinghy. He didn't have to wait long before he was drinking a warm beer.

Campbell phoned the Keevil base and explained what had happened. The base arranged for the crew to fly back.

At the base, a doctor examined Flight Sergeant Gladwin's eye. It was not injured. His vision problem, as Campbell suspected, was caused only by clotted blood.

The commanding officer at Keevil was interested in the crew's experience. He asked Campbell to tell other flight crews what had happened. The senior officer then spoke about the importance of practising ditching procedures.

Other airmen at the base had a different interest in the crew's plight. Some had lost various items, such as flying boots. They suggested to Campbell that he say he had lost them when he had to leave I for Item. The airmen wanted him to seek replacements, which he would give to them. Although chagrined by their requests, Campbell helped his fellow airmen replace their missing items.

———————◆———————

After his ordeal in I for Item, Ralph Campbell was never quite as confident as he had previously been that he and his crew could control every aspect of their fate. He became more aware that a crew needed good fortune, as well as good skills.

———————◆———————

Campbell was soon back in the pilot's seat. Promoted to a flight lieutenant, he continued flying with 196 Squadron.

On the night of February 21, 1945, he went on a raid to Rees, a town in Germany's Ruhr Valley. The only person in his crew who had been with him when he ditched in the Channel was McQuillan, the wireless operator. Some members of the old crew had been released from flying duties. Others were unavailable because of medical problems.

On this flight with Campbell and McQuillan were Flight Lieutenant Claire Bassett, the bomb-aimer, from southwestern Ontario; Warrant Officer Mick McGovern, the rear gunner, from Toronto; Flight Sergeant Doug Vince, the flight engineer, from Felixstowe, in Suffolk, England; and Flying Officer Peter Boddington, the navigator, from the Bristol area in England.

Flying in a Stirling with the call letters LX126, the crew dropped their bombs over Rees and returned to England. Up to that point, the flight had been uneventful.

Campbell was just above 196 Squadron's new base at Shepherds Grove, in Suffolk. Flying at only 600 feet (200 metres) above ground he could see the runway lights. The plane's wheels were down, ready to land. Campbell started to feel relaxed — the tension he felt when flying over Germany was now behind him.

Campbell's right hand adjusted the throttles for each of LX126's four engines. He slowly pulled them back, reducing the plane's speed to about 215 kilometres an hour. Then he saw sparks coming from behind LX126 and he heard a rat-a-tat-tat noise. The plane vibrated. Campbell didn't know what had happened.

"It's a Junkers 88," Bassett, the bomb-aimer, said, referring to the twin-engine German aircraft. It had fired bullets and shells along the port side of LX126, hitting the middle of the fuselage and the tail. The German plane probably arrived in England by flying over the North Sea.

"We're all on fire back here," McQuillan shouted on the intercom.

Vince, the flight engineer, expressed the same concern. "Fire down the back," he said. "I am going down."

Campbell hadn't expected an enemy aircraft to be over his base, particularly at this point in the war, when Allied troops were in Germany. Indeed, on this day the U.S. Third Army, led by Lieutenant General George S. Patton, took hundreds of prisoners as it marched through the Eiffel Mountains in western Germany.

With his plane on fire, Campbell had to think quickly. He knew he was just above the ground and his crew could not bail out. He would either have to risk taking the time to climb higher or he would have to bring the plane down immediately, risking the possibility of him and his crew perishing in a crash-landing. He also knew that the plane still had 400 gallons of fuel — more than enough to cause a massive explosion.

Vince, the flight engineer, walked back from his station to the midsection of the aircraft. Seeing flames, he picked up a fire extinguisher and aimed it at them. Vince was wearing thin silk gloves, not the thick leather gauntlets often used by air crew. He wore the silk gloves because, as a flight engineer, he had to keep a written log of the amount of fuel the plane had consumed. The extinguisher turned out to be exceedingly hot and it burned the skin on Vince's hands. It also failed to put out the fire.

Vince threw the extinguisher away and continued walking through smoke and fire. He found McGovern, the rear gunner. McGovern was supposed to be in the gun turret at the rear of the plane, but he had entered the fuselage. Despite the noise of the engines, Vince heard the gunner scream. He was apparently hurt.

Vince pushed McGovern forward because the front of the plane had not been on fire when he left that area. The smoke then became so heavy that Vince passed out.

———————◆———————

The officers in the control tower at Shepherds Grove realized that Campbell's plane was in trouble. They saw the German plane attack it and they saw sparks trailing behind LX126 like a comet. They told emergency crews to get ready to help the crew.

———————◆———————

Campbell decided that he and his crew had a better chance of surviving if he brought LX126 down quickly, rather than taking the time to fly high enough to let everyone bail out.

"Open the hatches," Campbell said. He wanted them open so that the hatch doors would not be jammed shut if LX126's frame twisted during a crash-landing. Bassett opened the escape hatch above Campbell. McQuillan, the wireless operator, opened the astrodome in the middle of the plane, which served as the central escape hatch.

With the hatches open, oxygen entered the fuselage, feeding the fire. Fumes, smoke, and sparks moved toward the front of the plane. Some of the sparks went right through the cockpit and out of the hatch above Campbell.

The members of the crew tried to get as far away from the fire as possible. Bassett, the bomb-aimer, sat in the co-pilot's seat. McQuillan and Boddington, the navigator, crouched beside the cockpit seats.

Campbell brought the plane onto the runway, but he couldn't see where he was going because the cockpit was full of smoke. He stood on the pilot's seat and stuck his head out of the hatch above him. The aircraft veered to the right, then went off the runway. Campbell returned to his seat, and applied the brakes. The plane stopped. He climbed through the escape hatch and jumped to the ground twenty-two feet (6.6 metres) below him. Bassett and Boddington got out the same way.

McQuillan climbed through the central escape hatch, went along a wing, and jumped to the ground.

With the help of the oxygen coming through the escape hatch, Vince regained consciousness. He still had trouble breathing, but he managed to climb through the hatch, walk along a wing, and leap to the ground. He joined other members of the crew.

Vince noticed that McGovern was missing. "Mick is still in there," he said. Others told him that McGovern had run in another direction.

They were mistaken. McGovern did not get out of the aircraft. He died in the fire and was buried at Brookwood Military Cemetery near London. He was twenty-two.

McQuillan and Vince both suffered from burns to their hands and faces. They were taken to the sick quarters on the Shepherds Grove base where their burns were bandaged. They then went to a nearby hospital and were later transferred to Queen Victoria Hospital in East Grinstead, a small town south of London.

Under the direction of Dr. Archibald McIndoe, the hospital had become famous as a centre for plastic surgery. Dr. McIndoe personally performed some of the skin grafts on Vince's right hand, the hand that had held the hot fire extinguisher.

Dr. McIndoe and his staff treated not only physical injuries, but also psychological wounds, giving hope to patients who were severely scarred and injured. Dr. McIndoe wanted the airmen to maintain their identity, and to feel that they could still live normal lives. To accomplish this he insisted, contrary to military tradition, that his patients be allowed to wear their uniforms in the hospital, and he encouraged them to visit residents of East Grinstead. He also permitted the men to drink beer, a "liquid medication" not available in most hospitals.

The patients formed what became known as the Guinea Pig Club, a self-deprecating name that reflects the fact plastic surgery was in an experimental stage during the war.

———◆———

On July 13, 1945, two months after the war in Europe ended, King George VI invited Campbell to an investiture ceremony at Buckingham Palace. The King presented Campbell with the Distinguished Flying Cross. The citation noted Campbell's courage and mentioned that he had successfully brought his plane down after it lost two engines. At the same time, the King also presented Campbell with a bar to go with the medal. He received it for his skilful flying after the ditching incident.

Campbell was surprised at the magnificence of the ceremony. He felt more at home in an Ontario farmhouse than in a palace.

Shortly afterward, he boarded the *Duchess of Richmond* at Liverpool, and sailed for Quebec City. He was on board the ocean liner on August 6, when he and the other servicemen heard that the Americans had dropped an atomic bomb on Hiroshima, killing thousands instantly and releasing radiation that subsequently killed thousands more.

Three days later the Americans dropped another atomic bomb on Nagasaki. Within days, the Japanese government surrendered. The war in the Pacific was over.

———◆———

Campbell returned to his family's farm at Foxboro, but the war had broadened his outlook. He decided to go to the University of Toronto where he studied economics, and then to Oxford University as a Rhodes Scholar.

Back in Canada, he became a lecturer and head of agricultural economics at the Ontario Agricultural College in Guelph.

Later, he served as an adviser to governments in Jordan and Kenya, and as a senior administrator at Canadian universities. In 1976, he became president of the University of Manitoba.

In 1990, while visiting England, Campbell went to Selsey, the town where John and James Lawrence took him and his crew after their ordeal in the Channel. The two fishermen were no longer alive, but Campbell met James Lawrence, a grandson of John Lawrence who was named after his great uncle. The younger Lawrence knew the story of the airmen who ditched their plane in the Channel. He showed Campbell the twelve-foot boat used in the rescue. Fishermen still used it, but only to take them out to larger vessels.

Campbell gazed out at the Channel. It was calm, not like the day he ditched I for Item. The years disappeared like the morning mist. It seemed only yesterday when he and his crew had come ashore.

Two years later, divers came across a plane in the Channel, not far from Selsey. They sketched it and checked Royal Air Force records. They concluded that the plane was I for Item, but that it was too badly damaged to be retrieved.

Long after the war, Campbell learned from Sid McQuillan that Mick McGovern, the gunner who died after the German intruder attacked LX126, had a habit of leaving the rear turret and entering the fuselage just before a plane landed. This meant McGovern was not in a position to see an enemy plane approaching from the rear. It also meant he was not plugged into the plane's intercom and wouldn't know what was happening in the aircraft. McGovern's decision to leave his post may have contributed to his death.

After Doug Vince recovered from his injuries, he left the air force and worked with automotive and engineering businesses, as well as a fuel company. Vince, who will be eighty-seven in 2010, now lives in Felixstowe

Ian Darling

Ralph Campbell in 2007.

in Suffolk, which isn't far from the Shepherds Grove base where the German plane fired at LX126.

Dr. McIndoe, the doctor who treated the airmen at Queen Victoria Hospital, was knighted after the war. He died in 1960. To Vince, Dr. McIndoe is "Sir Archie," a term that reflects his affection for the doctor.

———◆———

Ralph Campbell retired to Orillia, Ontario. He died in 2008, at the age of eighty-nine. Asked in an interview, a few months before he died, what he learned from his experiences that he would pass on to younger people, Campbell said they should ask themselves, "What can happen here, and if it does, what can I do?" In other words, take time to think things out.

The farm boy who became a pilot and then an educator wanted young people to be ready to deal with whatever problems they fly into during their lives.

14
THE LONG FALL

Sitting in the rear turret of Lancaster bomber KB834, Flying Officer Ben Marceau could see nothing but Allied aircraft and the bombs they were dropping. Marceau and other members of the Royal Canadian Air Force's 434 Squadron were participating in a massive daylight raid on Essen, in the Ruhr area of Germany.

It was March 11, 1945, about 3:00 p.m. At 21,300 feet (6,390 metres), KB834 was above the clouds that covered the industrial city of Essen and the railway yards that were the target of the raid.

Marceau, who worked for Fairchild Aircraft Ltd. in Longueuil, Quebec, before he joined the air force, wasn't concerned about German guns firing at KB834 from the ground or the air. He hadn't seen any German aircraft or ground fire that day. By this time in the war, the Allies

Ben Marceau in 1944.

had weakened the German forces.

He was, however, afraid that a bomb dropped by one of the many Allied planes above him could accidentally hit KB834, destroying the aircraft. Marceau's heart pounded. Adrenalin raced through his body.

Flying Officer Thomas Copeland, the bomb-aimer, released the bombs that KB834 carried: a 4,000-pound bomb, three high-explosive thousand-pound bombs, and six canisters that contained incendiary material. Copeland then spoke on the intercom to Flight Lieutenant John Fern, the pilot. "Keep a straight course," he said. "I want to take a good picture." The "picture" he referred to was a radar image of the damage the plane's bombs had caused.

"Let's get out of here," Marceau, who was twenty-four, said to himself. He wanted the navigator, Flight Lieutenant George Rowe, to set a course that would take KB834 back to their base at Croft in Yorkshire, England.

Then a shell from a German anti-aircraft gun hit KB834. Marceau heard an explosion. The plane disintegrated. Marceau was blown out of the aircraft. He was wearing a parachute, but he could not use it because he was unconscious.

Without a parachute, a man falls about 300 metres every six seconds. Ben Marceau was going to hit the ground in less than two minutes.

Wreckage from KB834 was scattered over a wide area just outside of Essen. All of Marceau's crewmates were killed in the explosion: Copeland from Dundalk, Ontario; Fern from Christopher Lake, Saskatchewan; Rowe from Toronto; Flying Officer Joe Latremouille, the wireless operator, also from Toronto; Flying Officer Gibson Scott, the mid-upper gunner, from Vancouver; and Pilot Officer William Jones, the flight engineer, from Liverpool, England.

After falling about 4,500 metres, Marceau regained consciousness. He was in the clouds with his arms outstretched. Marceau brought his right arm toward his body, grabbed the ripcord and pulled. He felt the strings to the parachute. They were tight. Although he had never bailed out of a plane before, he knew from his training sessions that the tight strings meant that the parachute had opened properly.

Marceau could feel a liquid dripping onto the left side of his body. He wanted to know if it was oil from the plane. He touched the liquid with his thick flying glove. When he brought the glove to his mouth and tasted the liquid, he realized it was not oil; it was his blood, which was pouring from his face. Marceau's left eye was injured. The bones near his eye were shattered. His jaw was fractured.

As he descended, Marceau left the cold upper air behind him. The clouds made him feel as if he was in a steam bath.

He passed out again, but only briefly. After he regained consciousness for the second time, Marceau could see with his right eye that he was close to the ground. He thought his luck had run out. Marceau, who had also flown with 425 Squadron, had returned to England after all of his previous forty-six flights, but he knew his days as a rear gunner were over.

———————◆———————

Marceau landed in a plowed field. When he tried to stand, his legs collapsed. He was weak, but he felt no pain because of the natural painkillers an injured body produces.

Marceau rolled onto his back to unfasten his parachute. He then crawled to the chute with the intention of hiding it, but in his weakened state he did not have the strength. Instead, he used the parachute to try to stop the bleeding on the left side of his face.

Not far from him, two older men were working in the field. At first, they appeared reluctant to approach him. They may have feared he had a pistol. He waved at them as a way of calling them over. He needed help. Marceau didn't know their nationality. They didn't understand English, French, or the few words of German he knew.

Marceau gave the two men the first aid kit he carried, along with his survival kits. From the first aid kit, they removed a bandage and placed it on his face. He was happy to let them keep his survival kits. He knew he wouldn't be able to use them because German authorities would soon detain him and take the kits from him.

Shortly afterward, two young Germans in green uniforms, along with another German who acted like a sergeant, approached Marceau. The senior German frisked Marceau three times, apparently seeking a pistol, but he was unarmed. The sergeant then wanted all the kits and, suspecting that Marceau had given them to the agricultural workers, he ordered the two men to give them to him.

The two young Germans then lifted Marceau, supported him by his elbows, and helped him to walk. The sergeant, who was behind Marceau, kicked Marceau's legs as they walked. The three Germans took Marceau to a military barracks used by flak gunners — the troops who had brought down KB834 — and left him beside a fence. The troops seemed leery of him. They just stared.

Soon, they brought a stretcher and placed it near him. He crawled onto it. The troops picked it up and placed it in a military truck between two rows of Germans. The truck drove off. While Marceau lay on the stretcher, one of the troops tried to remove a ring from Marceau's left hand. It was his wedding ring. Marceau and his wife, Marguerite, got married six months earlier on September 1, 1944, while he was on leave in Montreal. Marceau clenched his left fist to keep his ring on his finger. Then he lost consciousness again.

Marguerite Marceau lived with her parents at 6409 Molson Street in Montreal. She was visiting relatives in Quebec City a week after KB834's flight to Essen. Early one day a cousin phoned her to say that her mother was ill and she should return immediately to Montreal.

Instead, Marguerite phoned home and spoke to her mother. She wasn't ill. Marguerite realized, however, that her family had some unpleasant news to convey to her. She had breakfast, along with a glass of brandy, and took a train to Montreal.

The news that awaited her was in a letter from the air force: Her husband was "manquant a l'appel" — missing in action. She also received the names and addresses of the Canadian members of Marceau's crew so that she could communicate with them. Despite the letter she received from the air force, she never doubted that her husband was alive.

Marceau remained unconscious in the truck, which took him to a hospital in Essen — the same city his crew had bombed. There, German doctors operated on him, removing his injured left eye and putting a steel wire on his shattered jaw.

He did not regain consciousness until March 16, five days after his flight. When he woke up he was lying on a straw mattress covered with cloth. Several bedbugs were in his mattress, one was on his nose.

"Herr doctor," Marceau said.

A nurse looked in the room.

"Herr doctor," Marceau said again.

The nurse walked into the room. Marceau pointed to his right eye and said "good." The nurse nodded.

A doctor came in who spoke English. He explained what had happened.

The nurse re-entered the room. Using the few words of German he knew, Marceau said "essen," not because of the city he was in but because it means "to eat." The nurse brought black bread and jam, but Marceau could not eat anything because his broken jaw prevented him from chewing. Instead, he drank liquids.

The next day, a German flak officer visited him. The officer spoke English. He wanted to know Marceau's name and what had happened to the rest of his crew. Marceau gave his name, rank, and serial number, J19723. He also gave the names of the six other members of his crew. Marceau did this because he assumed they were dead. He didn't think anyone else could possibly have survived the disintegration of KB834.

This wasn't good enough for the flak officer. He wanted to know about the other four members of the crew. In seeking eleven names, the flak officer was apparently thinking of the larger crews of American bombers. Marceau responded in a joking manner. "They escaped," he said.

Several days later, an American army sergeant suffering from a concussion was in the same room as Marceau. Their peaceful stay in the hospital came to a quick end. Air raid sirens started wailing. The United States Air Force chose that day to launch another raid. Marceau told the sergeant to remain in his bed and to cover his face with a blanket. He hoped the blankets would protect them from glass flying into the room.

The raid lasted about twenty minutes. Marceau and the sergeant removed their blankets, which were filled with shattered glass. They left their room and entered a corridor. The bombs had damaged the second and third floors. Corpses lay all over the hospital.

The two men went down to a cellar. From there, Marceau and the sergeant used a ladder to climb through a broken window. They got out, but in their condition they couldn't think of trying to escape. They noticed people from the hospital were walking in the same direction. They followed, even though they did not know where they were going.

Marceau and the sergeant soon realized that the people they were following were going to another hospital, which was a few hundred metres from the one they had been in. At the second hospital, a janitor pointed Marceau and the sergeant toward the cellar, a safer place. They stayed there for about forty-five minutes, then they left. The entire area was filled with smoke from the raid, and the two men became separated. Marceau could see, however, that the second hospital was beside an armaments factory.

As he supported himself by holding onto the factory's doors, two German men wearing uniforms approached him. They explained with the help of sign language that the American sergeant had asked them to find Marceau, who was easily identifiable because he was wearing a hospital gown.

The two men took Marceau to a park where they left him sitting on a blanket. With the air raid over, the day was pleasant and sunny. The nurse who treated him in the hospital came by. "You Americans," she said in an accusatory tone, forgetting Marceau's nationality, but linking him to the Allied planes dropping bombs on German cities.

Marceau replied in French. He told her not to blame the Allies, Adolf Hitler had started the war and that Germans deserved what they were getting. The nurse walked away. Two older Germans, a man and a woman, approached Marceau. They spoke to him because they understood French. They also understood the history of Germany during the 1930s. "Hitler a été élu légalement," they said — Hitler had been elected legally.

———◆———

Ambulance attendants approached Marceau, carried him to their vehicle and drove him to a hospital at an OT camp near Essen. The camp's initials stood for "Organization Todt," a civilian and military engineering agency established by Fritz Todt, a high-ranking Nazi minister. Most of the patients in the hospital were ill or injured war workers. The physician who looked after Marceau was Dr. Otto Trush. He took a particular interest in his Canadian patient and wanted to protect him.

Not everyone was so helpful. A member of the SS — the ruthless Nazi military force — was upset that an Allied airman was in the hospital, rather than a prison camp. Dr. Trush, however, refused to turn over his patient. Instead, he put Marceau in a hut on the OT camp's grounds. The doctor came to see Marceau every day. Sometimes he brought a form of medication Marceau was happy to take: bottles of brandy.

While in the hut, other Germans came by and spoke to him in English. They told him they were not National Socialists, or Nazis. To Marceau, these comments showed that Germans knew the war was coming to an end.

Marceau remained on the campground for several weeks, until the American army came to that part of Germany. A French man at the camp told the Americans about Marceau. The army then sent a captain and a sergeant in a jeep to meet him. The captain explained that he could not take Marceau immediately, but that he would send an ambulance.

On May 6, 1945, two days before the war in Europe ended, an air force chaplain took a car through the pouring rain to Marguerite Marceau's home. He rang the bell. Her mother answered. "Marguerite, c'est pour toi," she said. Marguerite went to the front door from the living room.

The chaplain said he had news about her husband. She asked if he was alive. The chaplain said he was alive but wounded. A few days later she received a letter from the Defence Ministry confirming the information the chaplain had given, and promising that the ministry would offer him the best medical care possible.

The American captain did as he promised. An ambulance arrived to take Marceau to a field hospital in Germany. There, doctors rewired his jaw and gave him a blood transfusion. He was then transferred to several hospitals while on his way back to England. He arrived at a Canadian-operated hospital near Southampton on May 6, the day his wife learned that he was alive.

Marceau also went to Queen Victoria Hospital in East Grinstead. This was the famous hospital that specialized in plastic surgery. However, he stayed there only until a dentist had worked on his jaw. He would undergo more treatment when back in Canada.

Marceau boarded the ocean liner *Duchess of Richmond* at Liverpool, which was sailing for Quebec City. He arrived there on August 18 and took a train to Montreal, where his wife and her father met him.

———◆———

The Germans found the bodies of all of Marceau's crewmates. A report prepared by Britain's Royal Air Force said they were originally buried in a cemetery in Essen. After the war, they were reinterred in the Reichswald Forest War Cemetery near Kleve, Germany.

———◆———

From a military perspective, the raid on Essen that Marceau participated in was successful. In their book, *The Bomber Command War Diaries*, Martin Middlebrook and Chris Everitt say that the Allied planes hit their target and that Essen was virtually paralyzed until American troops arrived in the city. A total of 1,079 aircraft took part, dropping 4,661 tons of bombs. The two authors believe 897 people died. The Allies lost three planes. One, of course, was KB834.

———◆———

By the time Marceau arrived home, the war against Japan was also over, but his battle to regain his health continued for three years. He spent much of that time at Queen Mary Veterans' Hospital in Montreal, where he underwent twenty-five operations to rebuild the left side of his face. To do this, doctors used bone grafts from his hip.

Ian Darling

Ben Marceau in 2007.

Marceau went on to work with the Department of Immigration for twenty-nine years, as a guard and deportation officer. He also joined the Legion and served as treasurer of 425 Squadron's association.

Looking back on his ordeal in KB834, his experience as a prisoner, and his postwar surgery, Marceau said when he was interviewed at his home in Montreal, that he learned to persevere.

Ben Marceau died in 2008. To the end, he wore the ring that he almost lost in a German truck on March 11, 1945.

15
THE LUCKY GUNNER

On a cool, cloudy evening, Warrant Officer Andrew Mynarski, from Winnipeg, sat on the grass at the air force base at Middleton St. George in northern England. A member of the Royal Canadian Air Force's 419 Squadron, Mynarski and the rest of his crew were waiting to board their Lancaster bomber, KB726, for a flight to Cambrai in northern France. The crew was going to attack the town's railway yards.

It was June 12, 1944, just six days after the Allies landed on the Normandy beaches. The Allied air forces wanted to attack rail lines to prevent the Germans from reinforcing their troops.

Mynarski found a four-leaf clover in the grass and gave it to his crewmate, Flying Officer Pat Brophy from Port Arthur, Ontario. "Here, Pat, good luck," Mynarski said. Brophy put the clover in his helmet.

Brophy, twenty-two, and Mynarski, twenty-seven, were gunners in the crew of Flying Officer Art de Breyne, the pilot of KB726. Brophy was the rear gunner, sitting by himself in a turret at the rear of the plane; Mynarski sat in the turret in the upper-midsection of the fuselage. They were also friends who enjoyed going to pubs together.

◆

KB726 took off late in the evening. It was just one of hundreds of bombers flying to France that night.

German searchlights spotted the aircraft shortly after it crossed the French coast. To get away from the lights, de Breyne put the plane into a dive. Immediately afterwards, he climbed. The plane got away from the lights. De Breyne was about to start descending from 5,000 feet (1,500 metres) to get ready for the low-level attack when Brophy said over the intercom that he had seen a twin-engine plane, but he lost sight of it.

De Breyne reacted quickly. He didn't wait for the German fighter to reappear. He made KB726 dive again, but it was too late. A German night fighter fired three cannon shells that hit KB726. Two struck the port wing, damaging the two engines and setting a fuel tank

Pat Brophy in 1942.

The Brophy family

between them on fire. The third shell struck the fuselage between Brophy in the rear turret and Mynarski in the mid-upper turret. It hit hydraulic oil lines, spilling fluid that caught fire.

De Breyne ordered the crew to bail out.

Brophy's turret was turned to the port side, but he couldn't move it to enable him to enter the fuselage because the hydraulic oil no longer flowed. He pried open the doors just enough to reach for his parachute, which was in the fuselage. He then tried to use a hand crank to move the turret so he could bail out, but the handle broke. He was trapped.

Mynarski came down from his turret and saw Brophy just as he was about to leave the plane through the door on the starboard side. Mynarski crawled through the burning oil to the rear turret. His clothes caught on fire.

"Get going — you're on fire and can't help me anyway," Brophy shouted, and tried to wave Mynarski away.

Mynarski wouldn't leave. He used a fire axe to try to pry open the doors, but they wouldn't move. Then he used his hands. The doors wouldn't budge.

Looking dejected, Mynarski crawled back up the fuselage. He stood and saluted. With the noise of the plane, Brophy couldn't properly hear what Mynarski said, but he thought Mynarski said, "Good night, sir." Then, with his clothes and parachute on fire, Mynarski bailed out.

While Mynarski had been trying to free Brophy, the rest of the crew in the front of the aircraft got ready to leave. Sergeant Jack Friday, the bomb-aimer, tried to lift the door of the front escape hatch. The door flew up, striking him above his right eye and knocking him unconscious. Sergeant Roy Vigars, the flight engineer, realized what had happened. Thinking quickly, he snapped Friday's parachute on him and dropped him through the hatch, pulling the ripcord at the same time. Vigars followed Friday through the hatch.

De Breyne and two other members of the crew, Flying Officer Bob Bodie, the navigator, and Warrant Officer Jim Kelly, the radio operator, also went through the front hatch. Everyone was out of the plane except Brophy.

The plane descended rapidly, landing in a cow pasture near the village of Gaudiempré. As KB726 came down, Brophy saw the ground. He recited the Hail Mary.

The plane struck a tree, which sheared off a wing. The impact jolted the rear turret, opening the doors and flinging Brophy out. He landed beside another tree about ten metres away.

Brophy was dazed. He slowly moved his arms and legs to determine if he was injured. He wasn't. He heard several explosions in the wreckage. Shells and other debris scattered over a wide area.

———◆———

When he got up, Brophy put his parachute into the fire so that the Germans wouldn't find it. Then he started walking in what he hoped was a westward direction — west because it would take him toward the Allies in Normandy.

He did not go west, however, but he walked in a circle because his compass was not working properly. The needle responded to his revolver, which was in his belt. He put the gun in his belt behind him and started his westward journey again.

Brophy went through farmers' fields and wooded areas. After travelling a few kilometres, he came to the outskirts of the village of Pas-en-Artois. He walked through the beautiful property surrounding an eighteenth century white stone château. Once the home of an aristocrat, it had been converted into a school. He crossed a small stream near the edge of the property and was back in a field. At about 4:30 a.m., he came across a dirt path and saw three men walking on it. They were coming toward him. He crouched down.

The three men saw him, and approached him. Speaking in French, they asked if he was an Allied aviator. Because of Brophy's uniform, they assumed he was either British or Canadian. Realizing that the stranger did not understand them, the men used hands movements to ask if he had come down from the sky. Brophy gave them a positive answer.

One of the men, Paul Cresson, was a twenty-four-year-old resident of Pas-en-Artois. He went ahead of the other men, leaving them to follow at a slower pace. With the two French men escorting him, Brophy went to the end of the path, turned right onto Place André Verquin, and then left onto Place du Petit Marché. As he entered Place du Petit Marché, Brophy could see a three-storey red brick building at the end of the street. Although he didn't know what it was, Brophy was walking toward the German army's local headquarters.

Mynarski died of severe burns shortly after he landed. Vigars became a prisoner of war, as did Friday, who remained unconscious as he descended. De Breyne, Kelly, and Bodie became successful evaders.

The two men escorting Brophy did not take him to the German headquarters, but to a house on the street. It was the home of Marthe Cresson, the mother of Paul Cresson. He had gone ahead of the other men to tell his mother about the Allied airman. Madame Cresson spoke English, which greatly helped Brophy. She explained that Paul and another son, Pierre, were members of the French Resistance. They belonged to a group known as Voix du Nord. Paul, whose code name was Brutus, was the head of a cell with eight members. When he met Brophy he was returning home after pulling down telephone wires to cause communication problems for the Germans.

When not helping the Resistance, the family ran a fabric and clothing store. They put Brophy in an attic apartment at the back of their property. They liked to use the apartment because it was separate from their own house. This would enable them to deny knowing anything about Allied evaders found in the apartment. They buried Brophy's revolver and uniform in their garden so the Germans would not find them.

Later in the day, Cresson's wife Jeanne went to do some shopping. German troops spoke to her on Place du Petit Marché, the street in front of her house. The Germans asked if she knew anything about a plane that crashed, or the flyers who parachuted out of it. Reminding herself to act naturally, she said she knew nothing about either, a comment she had to make even though she knew that at that moment Brophy was in the apartment at her home.

———◆———

The Germans found the plane in the afternoon on June 13, but they did not remove the wreckage for about a week. Presumably the Germans had more important matters to worry about, such as the Allied army in Normandy.

———◆———

The RCAF sent a telegram to Brophy's parents, George and Eva Brophy, on June 14 telling them that their son was missing in action.

———◆———

The Resistance gave Brophy false identification papers. He became Paul Jean Mere, a student.

Brophy was not the only Allied airman whom the Cressons protected. At one point they also sheltered an American pilot, Lieutenant Cliff Williams.

The airmen were not completely confined to the house. They would go out after dark, walking with Cresson and his wife, as well as his two sisters, Marie-Louise and Cecile. The residents of the village believed the sisters had new boyfriends. While taking their evening strolls, they walked right in front of the German headquarters.

For security reasons, the Resistance moved the evaders to different locations. Brophy stayed at several homes in northern France. At one house, Brophy helped the Resistance to sabotage a bridge and other parts of the communications infrastructure.

———◆———

A British tank unit liberated Brophy on September 1, 1944. He and other evaders then went to several villages to celebrate the Allies' success in forcing the Germans to retreat. He flew back to England on September

12. The RCAF sent a telegram to Brophy's parents in Port Arthur to inform them that their son had returned.

When in England, Brophy filed a report that said how Mynarski had tried to save him. Brophy also returned to a pub he had gone to before his ill-fated flight on June 12. In the pub he saw Jim Kelly, the radio operator. "Pat, you're dead," Kelly said. The two men spent a long night together. Brophy recounted how Mynarski had tried to save him. Kelly told Brophy that he had learned from a French man that Mynarski died shortly after he landed.

Mynarski was buried in the Meharicourt Communal Cemetery near the city of Amiens.

In 1946, the RCAF announced that Mynarski had been awarded the Victoria Cross posthumously. The citation said, "Mynarski lost his life by a most conspicuous act of heroism which called for valour of the highest order."

Brophy wrote a letter to Mynarski's mother, Anna Mynarski, to say he was pleased her son's heroism had been recognized. He said he had been as close to her son as a brother. "I was scared that night until I saw Andy," he wrote. "Then I was cool and calm." Brophy added that he would always remember what her son did.

Brophy, who worked at a paper mill before he enlisted, left the air force after the war, but rejoined in 1951. The air force assigned him to a radar unit. He worked as an air-weapons controller, looking after fighters. He remained in the air force until he retired in 1967.

Paul Cresson still lives in Pas-en-Artois with his wife Jeanne. He will be ninety in 2010. The building in the village that the German army used as its headquarters still exists, but it is now a medical office.

The location where the plane came down is still a field where cows graze, just as they did in June 1944, but the tree that KB726 hit is long gone.

The Brophy family

Pat Brophy in the 1980s.

Mynarski's attempt to save Brophy has not gone unnoticed. A cairn has been erected on Gaudiempré Street, near the crash site, and a statue of Mynarski has been unveiled at Teesside Airport in northern England. The restored Lancaster at the Canadian Warplane Heritage Museum at John C. Munro Hamilton International Airport is named after him.

Pat Brophy died in 1991, at the age of sixty-eight. He never forgot how fortunate he was to have survived the crash of KB726, and he never forgot the gunner who tried to save him. A few years before he died, Brophy said he thought about Andrew Mynarski almost every night.

16
A STUDENT IN PARIS

In July 1933, the Italian government sent an armada of seaplanes across the Atlantic. Under the command of Italo Balbo, the Italian minister of aviation, the twenty-four planes were going to the World's Fair in Chicago. The seaplanes presented a stunning, unforgettable image. One person who never forgot was Pierre Bauset. He saw the planes fly over his home in Outremont, on the Island of Montreal. He wanted to fly in one of them. The son of Paul and Marie Bauset, Pierre was only nine at the time.

Almost ten and a half years later, on November 25, 1943, Flying Officer Pierre Bauset was ready to take off for a flight to Frankfurt in western

Pierre Bauset

Pierre Bauset in 1945.

Germany. Bauset, twenty, was the bomb-aimer on Halifax bomber LK967J, known by the nickname J for Jezebel. Members of the Royal Canadian Air Force's 431 Squadron, Bauset and his crewmates were scheduled to depart at 5:00 p.m. from their base at Tholthorpe, in Yorkshire, in northern England. The briefing officer at a pre-flight meeting warned the crew to expect heavy flak in the Frankfurt area.

The day had been mild and sunny with a few clouds. The flight to Frankfurt, however, was postponed to 9:00 p.m. The crew suspected bad weather over the city caused the delay.

Then the flight was delayed a second time. Bauset felt apprehensive. He decided to have his parachute harness adjusted. Finally, just before midnight, at 11:52 p.m., J for Jezebel took off.

On the way to Frankfurt, German searchlights spotted J for Jezebel. The interior of the plane lit up. Without the protective cover of darkness, the aircraft was an easy target for anti-aircraft fire.

Flying Officer Basil Passant, the pilot, put J for Jezebel into a steep dive. He spun the plane away from the lights. J for Jezebel was dark again.

With only five minutes to go before arriving at Frankfurt, the plane flew into flak. A piece of shrapnel slapped Bauset's right hand, but didn't seriously injure it. Another piece of shrapnel hit his parachute, which was strapped onto the fuselage. It put a small hole in the parachute. The flak, however, did not damage the aircraft. Passant flew onto Frankfurt and found that Pathfinder bombers flying ahead had marked the target. The pilot kept J for Jezebel steady.

"Bombs dropped," Bauset said.

Passant kept the plane on a steady course while a camera automatically took photos that would show where the bombs landed. He then started the long trip back to England.

Bauset felt relief. Flying at 21,000 feet (about 6,300 metres), J for Jezebel was moving out of the danger zone. He left the bomb-aimer's position in the nose and went to the co-pilot's seat.

After a few minutes, Passant told Warrant Officer Russell Jones, the navigator, that he suspected they were further south than their planned route because he had been manoeuvring the plane to avoid flak.

Jones was about to check the plane's position by using the stars to take an astro fix, but Sergeant Marcel Dugas, the tail gunner, said he thought he could see a light. Sergeant Douglas Burleigh, the mid-upper gunner, also looked. Burleigh wasn't sure.

For a navigator to take an astro fix, the pilot has to maintain a steady course. Passant, however, did not want to do that in case the light Dugas thought he saw came from an enemy fighter. He wanted to take a less-predictable course, so Jones never determined the plane's precise location.

Suddenly, shells hit the aircraft from below and behind. Bauset could hear them explode, despite the noise of the bomber's four powerful engines. He didn't know whether the plane had been attacked by ground fire or a night fighter.

The plane shook and rattled like a tin can filled with gravel. Small holes dotted the aircraft. One shell exploded near the nose, punching it in. A blast of cold air rushed into the plane. A fire started in the outer engine on the port side. From his instrument panel, Passant activated a fire extinguisher that was near the engine. When it failed to stop the fire, he tried to extinguish the blaze by putting the plane into a dive.

Passant took the aircraft down about 15,000 feet (4,500 metres). The fire went out. He brought the plane back to a higher level.

J for Jezebel continued flying. Then, after about twenty minutes, it was attacked again. The similarity of the attacks made Bauset suspect a night fighter in both instances.

Burleigh, the mid-upper gunner, could see a second fire and told the pilot on the intercom that it was spreading to the wing. Flames were shooting as far back as the plane's tail.

After a few minutes, at about 4:00 a.m., Passant decided that J for Jezebel was doomed. "We have to leave the aircraft," he said.

"What's the altitude?" Bauset asked.

"Fifteen thousand," the pilot replied. Bauset knew this was sufficient to enable him to fall freely for several seconds before he pulled his ripcord.

He clipped on his parachute — the one hit by flak — and opened the side door in the midsection of the plane. He watched Burleigh dive out and looked at Dugas, who waved to suggest Bauset go first. Bauset sat on the edge of the door and eased his way through. He pulled the ripcord and saw his parachute open properly, despite the hole caused by the flak.

As Bauset came down, the sky was clear but dark. There was no moonlight. Bauset hit the ground hard. As he landed, he saw what seemed like a small white cloud. He quickly realized it wasn't a cloud; it was the parachute of an Allied airman. The airman started to run. Bauset did not shout because he wanted to avoid attracting the attention of nearby residents, so he ran toward the parachute.

"It's me," said Bauset, who recognized Jones, the navigator. The two men had landed in a freshly plowed potato field.

Bauset asked Jones if he wanted to come with him or go on his own.

"You speak French so I'll stick with you," replied Jones, who came from Trail, B.C., and had only a limited knowledge of French.

Their first task was to hide their parachutes. Bauset tried to put his in a pond, but when it wouldn't sink he hid it in a bush. Jones buried his in soil.

Bauset and Jones started walking as far as possible from the area where the plane crashed. They knew German troops would be searching for them.

The clear sky enabled the two men to use the stars to orient themselves. They walked through fields until dawn, crossing railway tracks and coming to a small wooded area, which provided reasonable cover.

They slept on the cold, damp ground. After a few hours they woke up to see a low-flying German plane, a Junkers 88. Bauset suspected it was searching for him and his crewmates. As the plane flew by, he stood as still as possible.

Jones, the navigator, checked the maps in his escape kit. He thought he and Bauset were near the city of Arras in northern France. He was wrong. Passant, the pilot, had been right in thinking he had taken the plane far off its course. Bauset and Jones were, in fact, a few kilometres north of the village of St. Mesmin, which is about a hundred kilometres southeast of Paris.

Their plane crashed into a grove of poplar trees thirteen kilometres northwest of St. Mesmin, in the village of Maizières-la-Grande-Paroisse.

While hiding in the woods, Bauset became hungry. He started eating the nutritious tablets that were in his emergency kit.

All that Bauset and Jones could see from the wooded area were fields so they decided to walk back to the railway tracks they had previously seen. The two men hoped that the tracks would lead them to a village or town. They walked through plowed fields and found the railway tracks, but the tracks were too open and would not provide enough cover.

Eventually they came to an unpaved road. A van came along and Bauset and Jones tried to get off the road, but the driver spotted them, stopped his van, and approached them. He shook their hands joyfully and said he was happy to see them. Bauset gave the driver his cigarette lighter as a memento to remember the occasion. The driver, however, said he could not help. He drove off, heading north. His reluctance to help was understandable because he owned a garage that serviced German military vehicles.

Bauset and Jones decided they would be wise to go in the opposite direction and headed south. The two men quickly met a farmer on a hay cart. They asked him if there was a nearby train station. The farmer pointed them toward St. Mesmin.

The two men walked for another twenty minutes and came to the outskirts of the village. They met an elderly farmer in his farmyard. Bauset asked for directions to a friendly place. The farmer became agitated. He was frightened. "Non, non, non," he said. After Bauset calmed him, the farmer told the men to continue down the road, cross a railway bridge, turn right, and go to the first farmhouse on their left.

The farmer knew he was sending the men to the farm of Aline Cossard on Garenne Street; what he may not have known was that German troops were at the farm, searching for Allied airmen.

———————◆———————

Bauset and Jones arrived at the farm, which had twenty cows and grew grains, at about 6:00 p.m. The German troops who searched the farm had already left, but they were not far away. In fact, they were in a nearby bistro. Furthermore, German troops were billeted in a neighbouring house, also owned by the Cossard family.

When the two flyers walked into the middle of the farmyard, a farmhand approached them. Bauset asked if he could speak to the owner.

Mrs. Cossard came out of the farmhouse. Bauset told her that he and Jones were airmen and that they were in trouble. He asked Mrs. Cossard if she could help.

Without hesitating to think of the risk she was taking, she told the two men to go into the barn and that she would send someone to talk to them.

Several members of the Cossard family entered the barn during the evening. They said they would help the airmen as long as necessary.

They would try to contact the French Resistance, but they feared that the Resistance may not be able to help for several months because the Gestapo had infiltrated it. Many members of the Resistance had been shot or taken to concentration camps.

Bauset thought he and Jones should leave the farm as quickly as possible. He believed the Germans would be less likely to find them in a big city such as Paris.

The Cossard family provided the airmen with food and civilian clothes, and they also purchased tickets for the early morning train to Paris. Bauset offered to pay for the tickets with the francs he and Jones carried in their emergency kits, but the Cossards refused to accept their money.

That night, Bauset and Jones burrowed themselves in the hay loft and slept.

Jones woke up first. He had to search for Bauset, but found him deep in the hay. The two men then ran to the station, hoping they wouldn't miss the train. They were twenty-five metres away from the station when the train arrived. They climbed onto the last coach.

As the train went through the countryside, the sun shone brightly. Jones sat in the window seat, with Bauset beside him ready to talk to anyone who spoke to them. Bauset explained to passengers that his friend could not talk because he was a deaf-mute, but he could tell from their quizzical looks that they didn't believe him.

The train arrived about 8:00 a.m. at the Gare de l'Est, the majestic station on the east side of Paris. When the two airmen got off the train, they saw five German guards at the end of the platform. Three carried guns while two checked identification papers. Bauset and Jones didn't have any papers to present to anyone.

Bauset noticed that some passengers lined up in front of the guards while others, who may have known the Germans, walked around. Bauset and Jones followed the passengers who bypassed the lineup and walked out of the station.

They felt relief. They had been lucky. Bauset felt they were on an adventure, but one that posed risks. His strategy was to do nothing that would draw attention. The two men decided to walk to the Eiffel Tower.

Bauset remembered that some flyers in his squadron suggested that an airman evading the Germans could try to seek shelter in a brothel. When Bauset and Jones stopped for coffee at a cafe near the Eiffel Tower, Bauset asked one of the customers if he could provide directions to the nearest brothel. The customer scolded Bauset, telling him it was too early in the day for that sort of activity.

In response, Bauset said he had come to Paris clandestinely and that he had no identification papers. The customer scolded Bauset again. He told Bauset that he shouldn't reveal this information to him. The customer pointed out that Bauset didn't know whether he would turn him in to the police.

Chastened, Bauset decided not to seek a brothel, but to put his faith in the beliefs he acquired growing up in a Roman Catholic home. After Bauset and Jones finished their coffee, they went to the Jardin des Tuileries where they saw a priest walking among the flower beds. The priest declined to help.

About noon, they entered Notre Dame de Paris, the Gothic cathedral on Ile de la Cité beside the Seine. Jones stayed in a pew while Bauset entered a confessional box and spoke to a priest. Despite Bauset's confession, the priest quietly said he could not help.

Bauset and Jones found a convent and knocked on the door. The mother superior wouldn't help.

Bauset became concerned. It was past mid-afternoon, and the curfew on businesses started at 5:00 p.m. After that time, finding accommodation could be harder.

Bauset remembered seeing the Red Cross sign at an office on Malesherbes Boulevard and decided to go to it. He spoke to a janitor and explained that he didn't have any identification papers. He asked if he and Jones could spend the night in the basement. The janitor turned down the request.

The two men returned to the streets of Paris, but Bauset decided to go back to the Red Cross office. This time Bauset offered francs. Again, the janitor turned down the request. The men left, but Bauset did not give up.

Just before 5:00 p.m., Bauset and Jones went to the office again. As Bauset spoke to the janitor, a lively young secretary walked by. She asked the janitor what was happening. He explained that the two men wanted to stay in the basement and that he had rejected their request because he did not want to lose his job.

"Vous êtes aviateurs?" the secretary asked, suspecting Bauset was an Allied airman.

"Oui," Bauset replied.

The secretary told the two men to follow her. She took them to a jewellery store on Raspail Boulevard. The store had expanded the services it offered, at least during the war. It took the men's photos, which were to be used on false identification papers.

The secretary then gave Bauset directions to 22 Grenelle Street. He was to ask for Father Michel Riquet, a Jesuit priest.

Father Riquet welcomed Bauset and Jones when they arrived, and he arranged a meal for them. There were about twenty people in what seemed like a boarding house.

He told the others in the house that the two visitors were cousins from far away, but he smiled as he mentioned this relationship. His extended family wasn't quite as big as he pretended.

Father Riquet arranged for the men to have false identification papers. Now Pierre Bauset became Pierre Valentin, a student in Paris.

Bauset and Jones went to stay at separate locations. Bauset stayed in a student residence for a few days and then moved to an apartment near the university for a week.

Father Riquet also put Bauset in touch with Marie-Madeleine Davy, a professor at the Sorbonne who was part of the French Resistance.

Through her students, Davy knew families who were willing to help Allied evaders. Davy contacted Louis Marcus, who lived on Dunkerque Street with his wife and two daughters, Jacqueline and Claude. Jacqueline was a student at the Sorbonne.

Louis Marcus had a particular reason for wanting to help the Allies. He was partly Jewish. Because of his background, he had been forced to sell his leather business and he was restricted from going outside his neighbourhood. He was also supposed to wear a Star of David to identify him as being Jewish, but he refused.

Jacqueline Marcus met Bauset at the apartment near the Sorbonne. She brought him a basket of fruit and a bottle of champagne to make him feel part of the family. Bauset and Jacqueline then took the Métro to the Gare du Nord, a station near the Marcuses' home.

Indeed, Bauset was supposed to pretend he really was a member of the family. The Marcuses told anyone who asked that Bauset was a relative from the Berry region in central France, a region where the residents had an accent similar to his.

Because he spoke French, Bauset was able to leave the Marcuses' home whenever he liked. He went to see the French actor Sacha Guitry at the Théâtre de la Madeleine, and he also saw a concert at Les Folies Bergère.

At one point, however, Marcus suggested that Bauset leave for a while. He said he thought Bauset needed some time away, but Bauset wondered if Marcus really wanted his wife to have a break from the stress of looking after an Allied officer sought by the Germans. Bauset spent a few days at the apartment of a friend of Jacqueline's and then returned to the Marcuses' home.

One day, a friend of Jacqueline's suggested that Bauset might like to meet another Canadian from Montreal, Robert Vanier. They met and walked around Paris, seeing the Eiffel Tower along with other tourists, some of whom were German officers.

A few days later, Marcus told Bauset that Vanier worked with the Resistance and was going to try to help him to escape.

One morning in January 1944, Bauset left Paris with Vanier and another member of the Resistance, Yves le Hénaff. Vanier had been a private with the Fusiliers Mont-Royal. He was captured during the disastrous Dieppe raid in 1942, but he escaped from a train taking him to a prisoner of war camp in Germany and he returned to England. MI9, the British intelligence service, recruited him to work in France with le Hénaff, who had previously been an officer in the French navy. Their job was to help Allied agents and evaders get out of France.

The three men went by train to a secret location in France. Vanier, who was a radio operator, tried to receive a signal through his radio that a plane had arrived at an air field to take Bauset out of France.

The plane never came. Bauset and his two escorts returned to Paris. Bauset was not sure what he should do. Having left the Marcuses he was reluctant to return. He considered going back to see Father Riquet. Bauset wandered into a market near the Marcuses' home and happened to see Claude Marcus, the younger daughter. He explained what had happened. Claude knew what he should do: She told him to come home.

After two more days in the apartment, Marcus told Bauset the Resistance was going to try again to help him to leave.

———————◆———————

On January 17, 1944, Gerard Blitz, a Belgian resident, arrived at the Marcuses' home to escort Bauset out of France. Blitz was an acquaintance of Marcus. From Paris, Blitz and Bauset went by train, bus, and taxi to the French village of Collonges, which is near the Swiss border.

The family in the house where they stayed in Collonges gave Bauset Swiss money to take a tram into Switzerland, but he didn't need a ticket. Instead, he walked across the border, going under one barbed wire fence, over a second, and under a third.

Bauset entered a village that was a suburb of Geneva. A Swiss police officer approached him and asked to see his identification papers. Bauset told the policeman he was a British subject, but had lost his papers. The policeman said he would have to take Bauset to the local police station. At the station, Bauset said he had been a student at Collonges, but had come to Switzerland to seek refuge.

The story didn't impress the police. They suspected Bauset was an Allied serviceman. The police kept him at their station for a few days then took him to the British embassy at Bern.

Bauset's ordeal was over. The embassy sent him to stay with other airmen at a Swiss skiing resort.

The embassy also arranged to send a message to Bauset's parents in Montreal. Until then, Paul and Marie Bauset did not know what had happened to their son after he left Tholthorpe for Frankfurt.

Bauset remained in Switzerland until September 1, 1944, when he returned to France, going to Marseilles and then to Paris, which the Allies had liberated on August 25. While in Paris he stayed for a night with the Marcuses as an airman from Canada, not as a relative from the Berry region. On September 19, 1944, Bauset flew back to England, landing at the Royal Air Force base at Hendon, near London. He returned to Canada on the ocean liner *Mauretania* in December 1944.

———◆———

After meeting Father Riquet, Jones stayed with an American flyer, Ed Sobolewski, in a small room near the Sorbonne. University students brought food to the room three times a day. Some days were special. In early December, Jones received a bottle of wine. Bauset, while staying with the Marcuses, had arranged to send it to Jones as a birthday present.

On December 12, a young woman in the Resistance, known only by the first name Denise, came to help Jones and Sobolewski leave France. First, they were to take the Métro to the Gare d'Austerlitz, a train station, but the subway station was so crowded that they became separated. Jones and Sobolewski were still on the station platform when the subway coach Denise had entered pulled away.

Fearing they could be on their own, the two men waited. Denise, suspecting what had happened, got off at the next stop and returned to the previous station. Reunited, they continued their journey.

At the Gare d'Austerlitz, they met Gilbert, another young member of the Resistance. Gilbert was helping two American and two British airmen. The two groups boarded a train for Carcassonne in the south of France.

In Carcassonne, Denise and Gilbert were supposed to meet a guide who would take the evaders across the Pyrenees, the mountains that form a natural border between France and Spain. The airmen hoped to return to England from Spain.

When the men and their escorts got off the train they could see several armed German soldiers and an officer who checked the passengers' identification papers at the end of the platform.

Gilbert immediately walked in the opposite direction toward a washroom. The men followed and remained in seclusion until the other passengers and the Germans had left the platform. The evaders then walked out of the station.

Denise and Gilbert looked for the guide who was going to lead the men across the Pyrenees, but they could not find him. The evaders went to a church where they simulated prayer while they waited for the new guide to appear.

Their simulated prayer was not answered. The guide did not arrive. They went to a Red Cross building where they had coffee and then boarded a train for the town of Quillan, which was close to the Spanish border. The guide that Denise and Gilbert were seeking lived there, but they couldn't find him. Disappointed, the men abandoned their hope of going to Spain.

The group stayed in a hotel in Quillan overnight, then returned to Paris. Jones had to wait for another opportunity to leave France.

That opportunity arose on December 24, Christmas Eve. Some guides in the Resistance took Jones, who by this time was separated from Sobolewski, to Douarnenez, a port town in Britanny. German troops sat on the train near him during the trip.

Fourteen evaders and about thirty French men stayed in a shack on the outskirts of the town. On Christmas Day, after the 11:00 p.m. curfew, the men went in groups of ten to a bay where they hoped to board a boat. They walked through damp streets in stocking feet, in order to make as little noise as possible.

One group got onto a boat. The other men were hiding nearby. But the group on the boat found that it lacked sufficient fuel for a voyage to England. The men returned to their shack, again making as little noise as possible.

The French men left the shack to go to a nearby town. The evaders remained.

Two days after Christmas, a woman who lived beside the shack rushed over early in the morning. "The Germans are coming!" she shouted. "The Germans are coming!"

The men dressed quickly and fled into the woods at the back of the shack. By early afternoon, however, the Germans were no longer coming, and the men went back to their temporary home. The evaders were then divided into pairs and sent to stay at homes in Douarnenez.

Finally, on January 20, 1944, with stars shining brightly, Jones and thirteen other airmen, along with about thirty French men, boarded a fishing boat, the *Breiz Izel*. The boat set off for England in the middle of the night, silently letting the tide push it out to sea.

Someone on shore, perhaps a sentry, called out. The boat started its engine. Someone called out again. A searchlight was turned on, but quickly turned off. The *Breiz Izel* sailed out of the harbour.

While in the English Channel, the men on board became sick from gasoline fumes and high waves. Near the English coast a British motor torpedo boat approached the fishing boat. The naval vessel escorted the fishing boat into Falmouth harbour where the men walked ashore, exhausted from the voyage but happy to be free.

Jones then returned to Canada and served as an instructor at the air force station at Boundary Bay in British Columbia.

———◆———

The rest of J for Jezebel's crew also survived the war.

Sergeant Ray Nelson, the wireless operator, became an evader, successfully getting back to England. The other four became prisoners of war: Flying Officer Basil Passant, the pilot; Sergeant Doug Burleigh, the mid-upper gunner; Sergeant Marcel Dugas, the tail gunner; and Sergeant Bill Bennett, the flight engineer.

———◆———

All of the key people who helped Bauset also survived the war, except for Yves le Hénaff. Le Hénaff, who with Robert Vanier tried to help Bauset leave France, was arrested and sent to a concentration camp in Germany. He died en route.

Father Michel Riquet, the Jesuit priest who assisted Bauset when he arrived in Paris, survived, but he had a particularly onerous time. The Gestapo arrested him and sent him to concentration camps. When Father Riquet returned to France after the war, he became a popular preacher at Notre Dame de Paris, the cathedral where Bauset unsuccessfully sought assistance. Father Riquet died in 1993. An obituary in the *New York Times* said he helped more than 500 Allied airmen escape from France.

Louis Marcus regained the leather business he had been forced to sell because he was partly Jewish.

In their book *The Bomber Command War Diaries*, Martin Middlebrook and Chris Everitt report that 262 aircraft — one of which was J for Jezebel — participated in the raid on Frankfurt on the night of November 25, 1943. The book says because of clouds many of the aircraft did not release their bombs over the city. About eighty residents of Frankfurt were killed in the raid.

After the war, Jones became a pharmacist. He now lives in Surrey, British Columbia. Jim Armstrong, another evader, recently informed Jones that the guide who went by the name "Denise" was Denise Lenain, a student at the Sorbonne. Lenain became a social worker after the war.

Bauset left the air force in 1945. In the postwar years, he went into the advertising business, as well as financial planning. In 1955, Bauset joined the air force reserves, serving as a flight controller at a radar base and then as an administrative officer. Later, he became a member of the Royal Air Forces Escaping Society, which was established shortly after the war to help those who had helped evaders and escapers. Bauset served a term as president of the Canadian branch.

Ian Darling

Pierre Bauset in 2007.

On several occasions, Bauset returned to France to visit the people who had helped him during the war. On one trip in 1977, he also went to Maizières-la-Grande-Paroisse, the village where J for Jezebel crashed. While there, he collected scraps of metal from the plane. Elizabeth Harrison, secretary of the escaping society and a sculptor, turned the metal into an abstract sculpture of a Phoenix rising from ashes. Bauset, who will be eighty-seven in 2010, still has the sculpture at his home in Montreal.

To this day, Pierre Bauset marvels at the courage of the people in France who helped him. These were people who risked their lives every time they saw him. These were people who lacked the protection provided to him and other Allied airmen by the Geneva Conventions. These were people to whom he will always feel a debt of gratitude.

17
EAGLES AT WAR

On a clear, moonlit night, Flight Lieutenant Tom Lane steadied his Halifax bomber as he and his crew approached Krefeld, a city in western Germany. This was the night of June 21, 1943.

Warrant Officer George Darling, the bomb-aimer, was in the nose of the plane, looking through the bombsights and giving directions over the intercom to Lane, the pilot. "Left. Left. Steady, skipper." He then pressed the black knob at the end of the bomb-release cord and uttered the words Lane was waiting to hear. "Bombs away, skipper." The aircraft released incendiary bombs that created an inferno, and flares that lit up targets for other Allied bombers that were following.

Quickly, the skipper turned the plane around and started the return journey to England. The bomber, HR685, was based at the Royal Air

Steven Darling

Tom Lane's crew at the Royal Air Force base at Graveley, England, in 1942: (from left to right) George Darling, Roy Macdonald, Tom Lane, Peter Jackson, Jimmy Janes, Don Alexander, and Jimmy Rogers. Janes, a wireless operator, was not with the crew on its flight to Krefeld. His position was taken by Peter Balson.

Force station at Graveley, near Cambridge, where Lane and his crew enjoyed riding bicycles to the local pubs.

Taking the normal evasive action, Lane moved the bomber up and down, and from starboard to port. By doing this, he hoped to avoid coming into the firing line of German night fighters.

The clock had moved into the morning hours of June 22, when suddenly, at about 17,000 feet (5,100 metres), cannon shells blazed through the sky from the rear starboard side. A night fighter.

The first burst missed. Flying Officer Don Alexander, the tail gunner, could see what was happening. "Dive port, skipper," he said. Lane dived to port. The night fighter aimed a second burst of cannon fire at that side, hitting the port wing between the two engines.

HR685 shuddered and flames streamed out of the wing. Flight Sergeant Jimmy Rogers, the engineer, tried to extinguish the fire. A minute or two went by — the flames continued to stream out. "Bail out," the skipper said.

Lane gripped the control lever hard, holding the bomber on a straight and level course long enough for the members of his crew to put on their parachutes and leave the plane. On their way out, Darling and Flight Lieutenant Peter Jackson, the navigator, came up to the cockpit. They gave Lane the thumbs-up, then bailed out.

Within a few seconds, Lane realized he was trapped, held in his pilot's seat by straps that formed a harness. In order to leave his seat, he had to remove a pin that held the harness together. But it wasn't in sight. "I can't find my Sutton harness pin," Lane said over the intercom.

Flight Sergeant Roy Macdonald, the mid-upper gunner, had been near the cockpit for the flight instead of in his gun turret on top of the plane. The turret had been removed so the plane could fly faster. He was about to disconnect his intercom and go through the front escape hatch when he heard the skipper. Risking his life by remaining in the bomber, Macdonald went back to the cockpit and searched until he located Lane's harness pin. Only then did he leave the plane.

After giving the other members of the crew — Rogers, the flight engineer; Alexander, the tail gunner; and Flight Sergeant Peter Balson, the wireless operator — a minute or two to get out, the skipper crossed over the co-pilot's seat, went down two steep steps to the main deck and moved toward the escape hatch.

Before he could leave, his parachute partly opened. Clutching it, he scrambled through the two-foot-square hatch, not an easy task for a six-foot man wearing a bomber jacket. As Lane squirmed through the hatch, his leather gloves were torn to shreds.

The rear wheel skimmed over his head, just missing him, but he was out of the plane. However, below him, to the west, was a hazard for which he had no training: the North Sea. Lane, a prairie boy from a farm in Manitoba, couldn't swim.

Based on the plane's crash site, German war records show the pilot of the night fighter was Captain Hans-Dieter Frank, who was flying a Messerschmitt 110, a twin-engine aircraft. After firing at HR685, he flew off to search for other bombers. He found them. That night, he shot down five other Allied planes.

From the perspective of the Allies, however, the raid on Krefeld was successful, even though forty-four of the 705 bombers did not return. The bombers destroyed the centre of the industrial city. In their book, *The Bomber Command War Diaries*, Martin Middlebrook and Chris Everitt offer some grim statistics: 1,056 people killed, 4,550 injured, 72,000 homeless.

News of the raid rapidly crossed the Atlantic. Quoting the British Air Ministry, a June 22 Canadian Press story from London said the bombers struck with "one of the heaviest loads so far released on any German target." Flyers described the smoke from the fires as being more than five kilometres high.

Berlin radio did not specifically mention the Krefeld raid, but said the attacks on targets in western Germany were "terror raids directed mainly against the civilian population."

———◆———

The ground staff at the Graveley base quickly realized something had gone wrong on HR685. Marked "secret," the Operations Record Book noted that the plane left at 23:13, then said: "This aircraft is missing and nothing was heard from it after taking off."

Telegrams were sent to relatives of the crew. One that went to the bomb-aimer's father, Percy Darling in Newcastle, England, said:

REGRET TO INFORM YOU YOUR SON WARRANT OFFICER GEORGE WILLIAM DARLING IS MISSING AS RESULT OF AIR OPERATIONS ON NIGHT 21/22ND JUNE 1943 STOP LETTER FOLLOWS — OC RAF GRAVELEY.

Officers at the base sent letters expressing sympathy. One contained the names and addresses of the next of kin of all members of the crew, so the families could write to one another.

Back on their grain farm near Austin, Manitoba, Amos and Alice Lane were informed that their son Tom was missing in action. He was only twenty-two.

Amos knew that his son had joined the Royal Canadian Air Force and had been seconded to the Royal Air Force in Britain, and he knew his son was a Pathfinder. The Pathfinders had the particularly dangerous job of leading raids. With the best navigational equipment available, they marked the targets for other bombers. The Pathfinders were the eagles of the Allied force, a status recognized through a special badge shaped like the majestic bird. They wore it below their medals.

A veteran of the First World War, Amos Lane expressed in simple words the meaning of the messages he and his wife had received: "We'll never see Tom again."

———————◆———————

Through luck rather than any particular ability to manipulate a parachute, Tom Lane landed in a farmer's pasture near the Dutch village of Dreumel. He had, in fact, been farther inland than he thought when he looked down from the bomber. Hiding in a cornfield, he watched a woman from a nearby farmhouse milk a cow twice.

At about 10:00 p.m., he approached the house and knocked on the door. The woman, along with a man and teenage boy, appeared not to be completely surprised by his arrival. They may have known that the Germans were looking for airmen. Within minutes, however, the woman held a pitchfork in front of Lane and the man held a rifle. They marched him off to a village where the local authorities turned him over to the police.

The next day, June 23, Lane was taken in a German troop van to Amsterdam and placed in a cell. A German officer who spoke excellent English interrogated him. "We've been waiting for you," he said. "What took you so long?" Lane provided the information that prisoners of war are obliged to give: "Tom Lane," "flight lieutenant," "J-15834 R-80241."

Subsequently, he was taken by train from Amsterdam to the Frankfurt area of Germany for further questioning. The train travelled beside the Rhine, passing through Cologne and past beautiful vineyards on each side of the river.

When Lane and other prisoners walked through the Frankfurt train station, the guards pointed their rifles — not at the prisoners, but at German civilians who wanted to attack the airmen. The civilians knew that Allied air crews had destroyed many of their cities and that Allied bombs had shattered the windows of the very station the prisoners had just entered. What they did not know was that Lane and his crew had been above their city on a bombing raid just weeks earlier, on the night of April 10.

◆

After he parachuted into a field of grass, Macdonald, the mid-upper gunner, went to a farmhouse, banged on the door, and yelled until an old man put his head out a bedroom window. "RAF! English! Aviateur Anglais!" The old man got dressed and came out with his bicycle. He beckoned the airman to follow. "Police?" Macdonald asked. The old man shook his head. They went to a small house in Dreumel. The old man knocked on the door. A policeman appeared. The old man vanished.

The policeman and his wife offered breakfast, coffee, dry socks, and a pair of shoes. They indicated to Macdonald that they had called someone who could speak English. That person turned out to be another policeman. The second policeman asked what he could do. Macdonald said he wanted to escape to Belgium.

"I'm very sorry, but you can't go now," the policeman said. "The Germans know you are here and will come for you. And if you are not here, they will take twenty men from the village and shoot them." In similar fashion, all members of HR685's crew became prisoners of war.

◆

News that the airmen were alive filtered back to their families during the summer of 1943. Macdonald's parents received a telegram sent by the

British Air Ministry. It said a German radio broadcast on July 26 had mentioned that their son was a prisoner of war. Confirmation came later through the Red Cross.

The relief felt by the relatives when they learned the men were alive was overwhelming. Darling's father in Newcastle expressed his joy by sending ten shillings — half a day's wages — to the Graveley base to be given to the person who packed his son's parachute.

From the Frankfurt area, Lane, the skipper, was taken by train to Stalag Luft III, a prisoner of war camp for Allied air force officers near Sagan in eastern Germany, about 160 kilometres southeast of Berlin. It was built and operated by the Luftwaffe. The camp, which held about ten thousand men in several compounds, had barbed wire fences, watch towers, and guards with machine guns.

Lane lived in the camp's north compound. In an attempt to stay fit, he participated in athletic events as often as possible, and he became

Allied prisoners in a room at Stalag Luft III. Tom Lane is seated at right. Beside him is Don Alexander, the tail gunner on HR685.

known as a "three games a day man." The games depended on the season, but Lane might play cricket, rugby, and fastball on the sandy sports field inside the compound. The Red Cross provided the equipment. The prisoners could also walk around the inside of the compound, provided they stayed away from the fences.

Boredom plagued many men. To overcome it, many prisoners played card games such as Euchre and Bridge. Some played with Ouija boards.

Lane, like other prisoners, kept a log book that chronicled his life since he was shot down. It contained everything from the home addresses of prisoners he wanted to contact after the war, to a card from Prime Minister Mackenzie King, sending him Christmas greetings in December 1944.

Prisoners who were older and had gone to university set up classes in their specialty for those interested in studying.

The prisoners had a subsistence diet. Breakfast, for example, might be two pieces of black bread. When food was particularly scarce, it might be fried turnip. Lunch might be a bowl of barley soup. Dinner might be potatoes and a few slices of Spam obtained from the Red Cross parcels sent to the men.

In the spring of 1944, the north compound was the scene of the breakout that became known as the Great Escape. While the prisoners were digging a tunnel known as Harry, Lane served as a "goon watcher," someone who monitored the guards and sent a signal, such as closing a book, if one approached the hut in which the tunnel started. On the night of March 24, seventy-six officers escaped. The Germans caught all but three. The Gestapo shot fifty.

Lane was not at the compound when the escape occurred. He had been moved to a satellite camp called Belaria, about five kilometres north of Stalag Luft III. To him, what had happened to the fifty men was not an act of war; it was murder.

Despite the barbed wire, the prisoners had something their guards gradually lost: hope. After the invasion of Normandy on June 6, 1944, troops from Britain, the United States, Canada, and other Allied countries gradually moved from the west toward the heart of Germany. The Russians, whose country had been devastated by Nazi Germany, marched from the east, not far from Stalag Luft III.

The advance of the Red Army, however, posed an unexpected problem. Hoping to use the prisoners to obtain better terms during negotiations to end the war — negotiations that never did occur — the German government decided to move them away from the Russians. The prisoners didn't know where they were going, what would happen to them or whether they would live.

At 9:30 p.m., on January 27, 1945, the German guards at the Belaria camp ordered the prisoners to be ready to leave on thirty minutes notice, but the Germans delayed the departure. The prisoners used the time to prepare for their march as well as they could. They used blankets to make capes, hoods, and knapsacks, and they used any wood they could find to construct sleds. Lane and a fellow prisoner, Harold Sullivan, built a sled out of bed boards and Red Cross boxes. In it, they put food and cigarettes, the latter to be used to buy German farm products.

The prisoners finally left the camp at 5:00 a.m. on January 29. Snow fell through the bitterly cold air. At the main gate, the guards handed out Red Cross parcels, but Lane couldn't take one. His sled was already full. Lane did, however, have room to carry one special item — his log book.

On that first day, the prisoners walked twenty kilometres through the countryside, to a village called Kunau. Their accommodation that night, as it would be on other nights, was in barns. They cooked what food they had over small fires — if the guards allowed them out of the barns. After several days, the temperature rose. Frozen ground turned into mud and the sleds became useless.

On February 2, after walking about a hundred kilometres, the prisoners arrived at the train station at Spremberg. They were put in cattle cars, fifty men per car. Their destination was Stalag IIIA at Luckenwalde, just south of Berlin. Stalag IIIA was a massive camp holding about 25,000 prisoners. Upon arriving at the entrance, Lane and his colleagues spent much of the night standing in cold rain, waiting to be processed. They didn't move into the camp until 6:00 a.m.

———————◆———————

Some prisoners fared even worse. After being confined to several prison camps, Darling was forced to go on two marches. On the first, he walked about a hundred kilometres, from Sagan to Spremberg where he was transported by rail in cattle cars across Germany to Tarmstedt, near Bremen.

On the second, he marched 190 kilometres, from Tarmstedt to Trenthorst, near Lubeck. When barns were not available, the prisoners slept in open fields. If rain threatened, they erected shelters made of bushes and trees.

Macdonald, who had also been in several camps, suffered from asthma while being marched away from the camp at Fallingbostel, about a hundred kilometres north of Hanover. A horse-drawn cart took him to the sick bay at Lasahn. The sick bay was not a hospital ward, but the floor of the village hall.

The prisoners risked death not only from illness, starvation, and cold weather, but from the planes above them. Just after Macdonald and his colleagues crossed the Elbe River at Lauenburg, a wave of aircraft fired rockets and machine guns at them. Dozens of men were killed. The planes were Typhoon fighter-bombers of the Royal Air Force. The Allied pilots mistakenly thought they were aiming at German troops.

———————◆———————

Once inside Stalag IIIA at Luckenwalde, Lane found the conditions worse than at Stalag Luft III. The huts contained triple-decker bunks and were filled with bugs. There was little to eat. With Germany collapsing, both local food supplies and Red Cross parcels became scarce. The daily ration was a fifth of a loaf of bread, half a litre of soup, about six potatoes, and an ounce of margarine.

Lane became sick. Suffering from jaundice, his hands turned yellowish. There was no medication. A camp doctor advised him not to shower, so as to avoid losing body oils and vitamins through his skin. With the arrival of Red Cross parcels in mid-March, his condition improved.

A British intelligence report indicates that German guards left Stalag IIIA in the early afternoon of April 21, 1945, and that a Russian armoured car entered the camp at 6:00 a.m. the next day. Later that morning, Russian troops moved into nearby Luckenwalde in a disciplined manner, much to the surprise of the residents.

The Russians did not immediately free all the men in the camp. Russian authorities used the prisoners as hostages to make sure that Russia — technically the Soviet Union — gained control of Poland and that the western Allies lived up to an agreement they had signed regarding prisoners of war.

Josef Stalin, the Russian leader, wanted to make sure that the western Allies sent Russian prisoners who had fought on the German side back to Russia, where they would be dealt with harshly.

On the evening of May 6, an American convoy of trucks arrived at the camp. The Russians wouldn't let the Americans leave with any prisoners, and made their point the next day by firing machine guns over the head of the captain in charge of the convoy. Later that day, the captain came back with about five trucks, which he parked on the other side of a hill near the camp. He came into Stalag IIIA and started arguing in Russian with a Russian colonel.

Without waiting for that discussion to end, Lane, who had been walking around the camp, decided to go to the American trucks. He turned to two friends and said, "Let's go." With only the clothes he was wearing, he took his first step toward home, leaving behind a devastated continent. He also left behind an irreplaceable item: his log book.

All members of the crew of HR685 survived the war. Hans-Dieter Frank, the German night fighter pilot, did not. He was killed in a mid-air

Ian Darling

Tom Lane in 2008.

collision with another German plane.

Shortly after the war, the British government considered abolishing the eagle badge of the Pathfinders. The recommendation came from a committee formed by the British Air Ministry.

In his prison log book, Darling, the bomb-aimer, pasted a news story about this recommendation. Beneath the story are the last words he wrote in the log: "It's so easy to forget." After hearing from Pathfinders, the government allowed them to keep their badge.

Tom Lane returned to Canada and enrolled at the Ontario Agricultural College in Guelph, in the fall of 1945. Later, Al Studholme, a prisoner who had been with Lane at Stalag IIIA, visited him at the college. He had saved Lane's log book and brought it to him. Lane went on to become a professor at the college.

George Darling immigrated to Canada from England in 1955, moving to Guelph, Ontario, where his skipper lived. In 1960, Darling, my uncle, moved to Galt, where he remained until he died on November 7, 2002. His funeral was on November 11, Remembrance Day. The skipper, who will be ninety in 2010, delivered the eulogy, a poppy in his lapel.

Gertie Darling

George Darling in 2000.

THE SALUTE

Second Lieutenant Charles Brown, a twenty-two-year-old pilot from Weston, West Virginia, woke up early on December 20, 1943, to get ready for a bombing trip to Germany. He was a member of the U.S. Army Air Forces' 379th Bomb Group. Brown and his nine crewmates were based at Kimbolton, which is near Cambridge, England.

Their target that morning was an aircraft factory near Bremen in northwest Germany. Brown flew his B-17 bomber, which he and his crew affectionately called Ye Olde Pub, at 27,300 feet (about 8,200 metres). When they were about ten minutes away from the target, German anti-aircraft guns fired at them. The flak damaged two of the plane's four engines and put a large hole in Ye Olde Pub's Plexiglas nose, letting the -60°C air into the aircraft.

Charles Brown

Charles Brown during the war.

Ye Olde Pub started falling behind the other aircraft on the raid, and became easy prey for German fighter planes. Shortly after the crew dropped their bomb load, fifteen German fighters spotted the struggling aircraft and attacked from both the front and the rear. In a desperate attempt to escape, Brown turned Ye Olde Pub sharply from side to side, but he couldn't maintain control of the aircraft. Ye Olde Pub rolled over until it was upside down and started plunging to the ground.

At that point, the German pilots ceased their attack, apparently thinking the bomber was going to crash.

Brown lost consciousness, but regained it just before Ye Olde Pub would have crashed. Regaining control, he levelled the aircraft at an altitude of less than 500 feet (150 metres), but Ye Olde Pub could fly only slightly faster than the stalling speed, just below 160 kilometres an hour.

As he flew over the flat pasture land near Wilhelmshaven in northwest Germany, Brown just wanted to keep Ye Olde Pub in the air. He was flying in a northwesterly direction, trying to get out of Germany as quickly as he could.

Brown struggled with the controls. He particularly had trouble with the rudder pedals on the floor of the cockpit, which were supposed to enable him to turn the plane. The aircraft did not respond when he pushed the pedals.

Brown sent his co-pilot, Second Lieutenant Spencer Luke, who went by the nickname Pinky, and the upper-turret gunner, Staff Sergeant Bertrand Coulombe, who was called Frenchy, to check the condition of the plane and the fate of the crew. Although they could not see the full extent of the damage from inside the plane, the fighters had put hundreds of bullets and several cannon shells into Ye Olde Pub. They had damaged the tail fin, and destroyed almost all of the port tail wing and the rudder.

At least two cannon shells struck the radio room, knocking out the intercom and radio equipment. One anti-aircraft shell even went straight through the starboard wing without exploding. It just missed a fuel tank.

By this time, a third engine hit by fighter fire was not functioning properly, and only one of the aircraft's eleven guns worked. Ye Olde Pub was virtually defenceless.

The fighters had hit not only Brown's plane, but also several members of his crew. They killed his tail gunner, Staff Sergeant Hugh "Ecky" Eckenrode, and shattered the left leg of Sergeant Alex Yelesanko, the left gunner. They severely bruised the left leg of Sergeant Lloyd Jennings, the right gunner, and lodged a bullet fragment in the eye of Staff Sergeant Richard Pechout, the radio operator. They cut the forehead of Second Lieutenant Al Sadok, the navigator, and put a bullet fragment in Brown's right shoulder. Although Brown's injury was not serious, the intense cold froze blood and perspiration on his face, sealing his oxygen mask to him.

In addition, several members of the crew, including Pechout and Sergeant Sam Blackford, the lower-turret gunner, were suffering from severe frostbite.

Brown knew he still had to fly about 400 kilometres to get back to England. He also knew he would have to cross the North Sea, which in December is cold and rough, not ideal conditions in which to ditch his plane if he couldn't keep it in the air.

What he did not know is that Ye Olde Pub was moving into exceptionally dangerous air space: He was about to fly over the Jever Airfield, a bomber base used by the Luftwaffe.

———————◆———————

First Lieutenant Franz Stigler, a German fighter pilot, was standing on the airfield beside his Messerschmitt Bf 109. Jever was not his home base. A member of the fighter wing Jagdgeschwader 27, Stigler was based at Wiesbaden in central Germany, but he had landed at Jever to enable a ground crew to refuel and rearm his fighter. It was around noon, and Stigler was eager to fly again. He had shot down two American B-17 bombers during the morning and if he could shoot down one more that day he would receive the Knight's Cross, one of Germany's highest honours.

While waiting for the ground crew to finish, Stigler looked up and saw an American B-17 fly over a wooded area and then over the edge of the airfield. The bomber was so low he wondered if it had just taken off.

"Noch einer fuer mich," Stigler said — "Another one for me." He decided not to wait for the ground crew to complete their work. He climbed back into the cockpit and took off into the blue sky.

Stigler, who was twenty-eight, loved flying. He made his first solo flight at the age of twelve when he belonged to a glider club at the monastery where he was studying to be a monk. Later, he switched to studying aeronautical engineering and became a pilot with Lufthansa, the German national airline. When the war started, Stigler joined the Luftwaffe, serving as a pilot instructor. He volunteered to become a fighter pilot after his brother August, who was also a fighter pilot, was killed in 1940.

As the B-17 bomber limped along, Stigler approached it from the rear, his finger ready to fire if anyone on the aircraft pointed a gun toward him.

No one did. He flew closer, coming within six metres of the bomber. He

Franz Stigler during the war.

could see the damage to the tail and that the rear gunner was not moving. He could also see blood running down the barrels of the rear guns.

Then, he flew along the starboard side of the bomber. Peering through the holes in the fuselage, Stigler could see the crew in the middle of the plane attempting to help one of their comrades.

At that moment, members of the crew were trying to give morphine to Yelesanko, the left gunner, to ease the pain caused by his badly injured leg. The freezing temperatures, however, had turned the morphine into a gel that would not flow freely.

Stigler flew slightly forward so he was beside the B-17's cockpit. When Brown looked out of the starboard window, he was stunned. He never expected to see an aircraft marked with a swastika flying with him. The swastika annoyed Brown. It reminded him of Germany's decision to invade Poland in 1939, an invasion that started the Second World War. Brown felt as if he was in a nightmare. He hoped the German plane was just a mirage.

He closed his eyes for a moment, but when he opened them, the plane was still there. It was so close that the tip of its port wing was only a few feet away from the tip of Ye Olde Pub's starboard wing. Brown could see the German pilot's face, his eyes peering into the cockpit of Ye Olde Pub. The pilot, who appeared to be relaxed, nodded. Brown did not respond. Nothing in his training prepared him for this.

Brown wondered if the fighter was out of ammunition, but he dismissed this idea, realizing that an unarmed German pilot would not come close to an Allied plane. He also wondered if the fighter carried a secret weapon that would destroy his plane, but no such weapon emerged.

Brown knew nothing about the German pilot's motives, but he did see the pilot point down with his hand. He knew what that meant. The pilot wanted him to land. Brown just kept flying. He was not going to surrender. The German pilot then nudged his fighter ahead of the bomber a few times, again trying to get the American pilot to land. Again, Brown refused. Then, the German pilot pointed toward the northeast, but Brown did not understand what message he intended to convey. Brown continued flying. By this time, Ye Olde Pub was no longer over mainland Germany, but was over the North Sea.

Pinky, the co-pilot, and Frenchy, the upper-turret gunner, returned to the cockpit. The two men saw the German fighter. They, too, were stunned.

After a few minutes, Brown wanted to end the encounter. Flying beside an enemy aircraft made him feel tense. "Get up there and scare that bandit away," Brown said to Frenchy, urging the gunner to return to his turret to point his gun at the fighter.

Brown turned Ye Olde Pub in a westerly direction that would take it toward England. He looked again at the German plane and, much to his amazement, the pilot gave him a friendly salute. The fighter then dived to the right and disappeared.

Brown managed to get Ye Olde Pub up to about 1,000 feet (300 metres). He stayed close to the islands off the German coast, just in case he had to make a crash landing.

He checked with his crew to see if anyone wanted him to fly back to Germany so they could bail out. No one did. All members of the crew who were not injured chose to stay on board to look after those who were wounded, and to help Brown fly the plane. They were a crew. They had trained together and they were going to stay together.

When Brown had flown parallel to the islands as far as he could, he turned and headed directly for northeast England.

Ye Olde Pub gradually lost altitude. The needle on the altimeter showed that the aircraft had gone below 1,000 feet. Brown had a good view of the North Sea. It was dull and grey, except for the whitecaps, which meant strong waves were rolling across the sea. Ditching would be difficult.

Brown ordered the crew to throw anything that was movable overboard to lighten the load. They threw guns, ammunition, oxygen equipment, and parts of the radio system that had been destroyed.

The needle pointed to 500 feet, then 400 feet.

As he flew, he saw other bombers high above him on their way back from Germany. He envied them.

Several P-47 Thunderbolts flew close to him. These American fighter planes waggled their wings to show the pilot of the bomber they were aware of his plight. Brown hoped the fighters had alerted Air-Sea Rescue units. By this time, Brown was relying on more than his training and his experience; he was praying. He desperately wanted to see land.

The needle pointed to 300 feet.

Then, at about 250 feet (75 metres) Brown saw something on the horizon. It was a rocky shore. It was England.

Soon, a P-47 appeared on each side of Ye Olde Pub, flew over the coast, climbed to about 1,000 feet, and began to circle. They were trying to draw Brown's attention to the land beneath them. When Brown looked in the direction they indicated, he realized they were above an airfield. He lightly rocked Ye Olde Pub's wings to thank the P-47s for their help.

One of the airfield's runways lined up with Ye Olde Pub's course.

"Gear down," Brown said to Frenchy, referring to the landing gear. The wheels went down. As they approached the runway, Brown and Pinky, the co-pilot, either shut down or cut power to all the engines, and Ye Olde Pub glided to a safe landing. Charles Brown's prayers were answered.

——————◆——————

Back in Germany, Stigler had returned to the Jever base. He said nothing to anyone about the American bomber. He was worried. He knew that senior Luftwaffe officers would court-martial him if they knew he had deliberately failed to shoot down an American bomber. The penalty could be severe: He might be shot.

——————◆——————

Ye Olde Pub had landed at the Seething airbase near Great Yarmouth on England's east coast. This was the home of the American 448th Bomb Group, which flew B-24 bombers.

Brown dropped down through the hatch in the front of the aircraft and slumped to the tarmac. Three injured airmen — Yelesanko, Pechout, and Blackford — were helped out and taken away by ambulance. Hugh Eckenrode's body was removed.

The medics tried to get Brown onto a stretcher. "You're wounded," one of them said.

"No I'm not," he replied, and then he and the rest of the crew were taken to a debriefing session. After that, Colonel James M. Thompson, commander of the 448th Bomb Group, took Brown back to the aircraft. Brown couldn't believe what he saw. When he looked at the tail — or rather what was left of it — he realized why he hadn't been able to control the plane.

Thompson then said, "Lieutenant, why would you try to fly an aircraft damaged this badly?"

"Sir," Brown replied, "I had one already dead and three who could not survive a bail out, and besides I did not know that the tail had been shot off the aircraft."

"Young man," the colonel said, "I'm going to recommend you for our nation's highest award." Although still in shock, Brown assumed Thompson was referring to the Medal of Honor. Brown asked about the crew, and Thompson said they would be taken care of. Brown assumed his crewmates would receive official recognition for what they had done.

Within hours of Ye Olde Pub landing at Seething, base officials classified the aircraft as secret. Film of all photos taken of the plane was confiscated. A telegram that the Seething base sent to the crew's home base at Kimbolton said nothing about an encounter with a German pilot. When the crew returned to Kimbolton, no one spoke to them about their ordeal.

Staff Sergeant Hugh Eckenrode, the rear gunner, was posthumously awarded the Distinguished Flying Cross, but neither Brown nor his crew received official recognition for what they had achieved by flying Ye Olde Pub back to England.

The war continued. A few weeks after Ye Olde Pub landed at Seething, Brown flew again on a different bomber. He was joined by his crewmates who were not injured, Blackford, who returned to active duty after being in hospital for two weeks, and flyers who replaced Eckenrode, Pechout, and Yelesanko, whose leg was amputated.

Brown completed his last combat flight on April 11, 1944. Then, operating from Northern Ireland, he ferried American planes around Great Britain. He was too busy to think about his encounter with the German pilot.

In mid-August of 1944, he boarded a ship to return to the United States. As he sailed into New York, he saw a sight that symbolized what he had been fighting for: the Statue of Liberty.

Franz Stigler was not court-martialled because no one knew what he had done. He continued to fly, joining the Jagdverband 44 squadron. This elite group of pilots flew the Messerschmitt Me 262, a new jet fighter. When the war ended in May 1945, Stigler was stationed at a German base near Salzburg, Austria.

After returning to civilian life in Germany, he worked for a branch of the Messerschmitt company that made knitting looms. Postwar Germany was a dreary country, particularly for an energetic man such as Stigler. He decided to leave. In 1953 he emigrated to Canada where he had a relative. He hoped to work on an innovative Canadian fighter plane, the Avro Arrow. After arriving in Canada, Stigler found that he would have to live in the country for two years before he could work on the Arrow, because it was a military plane.

He didn't want to wait so he went to the Queen Charlotte Islands in British Columbia where he worked in the truck and boat repair shop of a logging company. After living in several other communities in the province, he moved to a large treed lot in the Vancouver suburb of Surrey in 1971.

Brown went to West Virginia Wesleyan College, and upon graduation in 1949 he rejoined the U.S. Air Force. He primarily served in the intelligence and counter-intelligence fields. He took early retirement in 1965, and become a diplomat with the State Department. When he retired in 1972, Brown moved to Miami where he set up an energy and environmental research company. In the postwar years, his encounter with the German pilot faded in his memory.

In 1986 while attending a reunion of air force veterans in Las Vegas, organized by the Air Force Association, Brown was at a table where former flyers were chatting about unusual incidents they had been involved in or seen. When his turn came, Brown said a German pilot once saluted him. The group laughed, but they were intrigued.

Brown decided to see if he could find out who the pilot was, whether he survived the war, and why he didn't shoot down Ye Olde Pub. He searched records of the 448th Bomb Group, stories that appeared in British newspapers, and museums in both England and the United States. He found nothing. He contacted German historians, but there were no records in Germany because Stigler never told anyone what he had done.

In the fall of 1989, Brown submitted a letter to *Jagerblatt*, a newsletter sent to Luftwaffe pilots, asking if anyone knew about his flight of December 20, 1943. A few months later, four years after he started searching for the German pilot, Brown received an envelope with a Canadian stamp. It contained a letter from Franz Stigler. "I was the one," Stigler wrote.

Brown called directory assistance for the Vancouver area, received Stigler's phone number then called him. "Convince me," Brown said to Stigler.

Stigler did precisely that. He told Brown the location, and he described the encounter, the condition of the plane, and the aircraft's markings, such as the "K" painted on the tail which was the letter of the 379th Bomb Group.

"It has to be you," Brown said.

Charles Brown arranged to meet Franz Stigler in 1990, in Seattle. He then learned the full details of Stigler's flight. Stigler's fighter was fully armed, but he chose not to shoot down Ye Olde Pub because it was so badly damaged. He had never seen a plane flying in such a condition. He thought firing at an *Charles Brown in 2007.*

Ian Darling

Ian Darling

Franz Stigler in 2007.

aircraft in that condition would be like firing at a man in a parachute. Stigler also explained that when he pointed to the northeast, he wanted the plane to fly to Sweden, a neutral country.

When Stigler couldn't get the plane to land, he thought the pilot was crazy. He didn't think it would be able to fly back to England.

Brown and Stigler subsequently became close friends, visiting each other and talking on the phone every week. With Brown's assistance, Stigler became an honorary member of the 379th Bomb Group and received several humanitarian awards. He was also honoured by veterans' organizations.

Brown, who will be eighty-eight in 2010, thinks the air force chose to ignore his flight because it did not want to give any publicity to a crew whose lives were spared by a German pilot.

In 2008, however, the American military finally acknowledged what Brown and his crew achieved on December 20, 1943. It awarded the Air Force Cross to Brown, in recognition of his extraordinary heroism, and the Silver Star to his crew for their gallantry.

———◆———

Franz Stigler died in 2008, at the age of ninety-two. His decision to let Ye Olde Pub continue flying ultimately meant he could show the world something more important than the Knight's Cross he would have received for shooting it down. He provided an example of honour in combat and the hope that today's combatants may become tomorrow's friends.

19
A PLANE FOR TOMORROW

With a Thermos of coffee to drink later, Flight Sergeant Thomas Weightman sat in the gunner's turret at the rear of a Halifax bomber. He and his five crewmates, members of the Royal Air Force's 644 Squadron, were ready for another trip from their base at Tarrant Rushton in southern England. They were flying to Norway. Their mission was to drop supplies to members of the Norwegian Resistance, who were fighting the Germans occupying their country.

It was April 23, 1945, a warm, sunny day with a few clouds. The winds were light. It seemed like a good day to fly.

Flight Lieutenant Alexander Turnbull, the pilot, took off at 7:51 p.m. The bomber, which had the serial number NA337, flew north, passed over Denmark, then headed for Mikkelsberget, a large hill near the

Thomas Weightman

Thomas Weightman during the war.

town of Grue in southeastern Norway.

Asjorn Furu Berg, a platoon leader in the Resistance, was waiting with his colleagues at the hill. The previous day he had received a coded message through a BBC radio broadcast: "Tyven assurerer mot innbrudd," which in English meant, "The burglar is insuring against burglary." The code informed Berg that a plane would be dropping supplies the next evening.

NA337 approached. Berg flashed a signal with a lamp to tell Turnbull he was in the right location. The bomber dropped the supplies and headed home.

At 1:30 a.m., the plane was about to fly over the Minnesund Bridge at the south end of the largest lake in Norway, Lake Mjosa. It was an important road and rail link between Oslo and Trondheim. A German anti-aircraft crew was at the bridge, watching for Allied planes. It heard NA337 and fired. One bullet put a twenty-millimetre hole in the middle of the starboard wing, right beside a main fuel tank. From his rear turret, Weightman could see sparks flying back from near the outer engine.

"Should I fire back?" Weightman asked Turnbull over the intercom.

"No. Don't do it," the pilot replied. "They could probably see us better."

"They can see us now," the gunner said, referring to the sparks, but he did not fire back.

Turnbull knew NA337 was in trouble. "Dinghy! Dinghy! Ditch! Ditch!" he shouted into the intercom.

These words told the other five crew members to prepare themselves to ditch on the lake and get into the dinghy.

The crew shut down the outer starboard engine and "feathered" the propeller, which changed the angle of the blade to reduce air resistance. Turnbull took the aircraft in a northerly direction, flying over farms and a forest close to Lake Mjosa. He then turned the bomber around so that when it came down it would be flying into the wind.

While Turnbull was deciding exactly where to ditch the bomber, Tore Marsoe, a sixteen-year-old boy, was lying in bed in his home just outside of Hamar, a city on the shore of the lake. The sound of the bomber woke him up. The engines were throbbing and he knew that the aircraft was in trouble.

The crew members got into their crash positions. Weightman moved from his turret to the middle of the aircraft and crouched with his head down.

The landing was rough. When the bomber hit the water, its nose shattered and the tail, including the rear turret, separated from the fuselage.

The other members of the crew scrambled to get out, but the impact of the bomber hitting the water threw Weightman to the floor. He lay there unconscious. Freezing water seeped in. Ironically, this helped him. It splashed on his face, bringing him back to consciousness.

When he was alert again, he could see that the turret and tail were no longer part of the plane. He walked to the rear to see if he could spot the dinghy that the plane carried in the port wing. A water-sensitive switch in the nose of the bomber was supposed to release and inflate the dinghy when the nose became immersed in water.

Weightman couldn't see the dinghy. It was still in the wing because the switch had been destroyed along with other parts of the nose.

Weightman hurried to the middle of the plane to pull a handle that manually released the dinghy. He scrambled back to the rear. He had released the dinghy, but when it hit the water it was upside down. He took off his shoes, jumped into the water, swam to the dinghy, and climbed on to it.

It was now early in the morning of April 24. A mist had formed above the lake. Through it, Weightman could see some of his colleagues in the water.

"Help!" he called out, hoping to hear a response from Turnbull, the pilot; Flight Lieutenant Walter Mitchell, the navigator; Flight Sergeant Goronwy Bassett, the flight engineer; Flight Sergeant Gordon Tuckett, the bomb-aimer; or Flight Sergeant Alec Naylor, the wireless operator.

Weightman heard only silence. His colleagues were dead. Except for Bassett, whose body was never found, the crewmates had managed to get out of the plane before him. But without the protection of the dinghy, they died in the icy water.

Weightman was alone. He was cold and wet, but he was not injured. A blacksmith from the rugged Northumbrian area of northern England, Weightman felt certain he would survive. To ensure that he didn't succumb to the cold, he stayed awake all night.

While he drifted in the dinghy, NA337 quietly slipped away, settling on the muddy bottom on Lake Mjosa, 240 metres below the surface.

———————◆———————

At dawn the same day, Kare Lovli, a Finnish citizen who had fled his native country to stay on a Norwegian farm during the war, was walking on the shore of the lake. Suddenly, he spotted something unusual. It was a yellow dinghy with someone in it. Lovli quickly found a rowboat and went out to rescue the person.

Lovli helped Weightman get into the rowboat, then returned to shore and took him to a nearby farmhouse owned by Engebert and Karen Vethammer. They gave Weightman porridge and dry clothes, and placed him beside a wood-burning stove. Karen Vethammer rubbed his feet to help restore the circulation.

While the Vethammers were still caring for him, Weightman looked out of a window and saw German troops coming to the farmhouse. Someone who knew what was happening had contacted the German authorities. The troops entered the house and confronted Weightman. "You're in the hands of the Resistance," one of the Germans said in English. No, he argued, telling them that this was just the house where he had been taken by the person who rescued him.

The troops took him in a motorcycle sidecar to a nearby German Air Force base, and later by car to Fornebu airbase near Oslo. The Germans were also holding two other Royal Air Force flyers at the base. Weightman had a jail cell there, but his stay at the base was not overly onerous. He was treated well and allowed to walk around during the day.

The Germans knew that the war was coming to an end. They knew that their side had lost and that Thomas Weightman and hundreds of thousands of other Allied service men and women had won. They did not want to be accused of treating Allied prisoners badly.

In fact, an armistice was about to come into effect. Weightman was at the base on the morning of May 7, when two senior British Air Force officers and several journalists in Copenhagen decided to fly to Oslo to see what was happening in Norway. They had access to a Dakota transport plane and departed for Fornebu airport. This was a risky flight because it was possible that some German troops in Norway didn't know about the armistice.

As the plane approached the base, the Germans flashed a red light, warning the pilot not to land. The pilot ignored it and brought the plane down. When the British officers disembarked, the German officers decided to surrender. They preferred to give themselves up to the British rather than to the more ruthless Russians who might be on their way.

The Germans also released their three prisoners of war. Weightman and the other two flyers were free. They returned to Britain on the Dakota.

———————◆———————

With the exception of Flight Sergeant Bassett, the flight engineer whose body was never found, Weightman's colleagues were buried in a churchyard at Hamar. In mid-May, the Norwegians held a military ceremony at the churchyard to honour the men. Their bodies were later taken to a military cemetery at Lillehammer.

Tore Marsoe, the boy who heard the bomber, attended the ceremony. He would never forget the bomber or the throbbing sound it made.

———————◆———————

The war against Germany was over. Weightman resumed his career as a blacksmith in the village of Longhoughton Alnwick, near Newcastle-on-Tyne in northern England.

The allies divided Germany into two sections that remained apart until 1990. West Germany underwent a phenomenal transformation to become a democratic society. East Germany stagnated under indirect control by the Russians.

While Weightman and other airmen who survived the war became middle-aged and then grey-haired gentlemen, NA337 remained in Lake Mjosa — cold, dark, and deep.

Years went by, and most people forgot about NA337, but not Tore Marsoe. He and a friend, Rolf Liberg, knew that the bomber was at the bottom of the lake.

In 1965, they started seeking information about the plane. In 1982, with the help of British museum officials, they contacted Weightman and arranged for him and his wife, Dorothy, to go to Lake Mjosa. Then, with the help of sonar equipment, they found the plane, but they couldn't find anyone willing to pay to bring it to the surface.

While Weightman was in Norway, King Olav V, on behalf of Norwegians, presented him with a certificate of appreciation for his role in liberating their country. During the same trip, Weightman went to see his old jail cell at Fornebu airport. He laughed when he saw it. The cell was being used for a non-military purpose: It was a maid's broom closet.

In 1993, Karl Kjarsgaard, an airline pilot from Ottawa, and a few former members of the Royal Canadian Air Force met in Toronto to find ways to tell Canadians about Halifax bombers, and the thousands of Canadian airmen who flew on them during the war.

Kjarsgaard had heard about a Halifax that ditched on Lake Mjosa. In February 1994, during a short stay in Europe, Kjarsgaard went to the Norwegian archives in Oslo, which put him in contact with Marsoe and Liberg.

They met Kjarsgaard at a hotel in Oslo and realized that he was serious about finding and restoring a Halifax. They showed him a sonar picture of NA337.

Kjarsgaard returned to Canada to tell the members of the group about the bomber. They formed the Halifax Aircraft Association and selected Jeff Jeffery of Toronto, a Halifax pilot during the war, as its president.

The association obtained permission from the Norwegian government to salvage the bomber. Weightman also gave his blessing for the project, as did relatives of Bassett, the crew member whose body wasn't found. Their permission was important because of the possibility that Bassett's body could be trapped in the aircraft.

The association hired Dacon Sub Sea, a company in Oslo, to bring the two sections of the bomber to the surface. Working from a barge, Dacon's plan was to use a vice-like piece of equipment to grip the rear section, and a huge fork-like device, nicknamed Moby Grip, to lift the main section. It would then lift the sections to the surface with cables. A remote-controlled submarine with two video cameras enabled the Dacon crew to see what was happening.

Dacon brought up the rear section, including the gunner's turret, on August 15, 1995. Weightman's Thermos was still inside the turret.

On August 21, Weightman arrived from England. At a dinner one

Thomas Weightman

NA337 after it was retrieved from Lake Mjosa in Norway.

night, Jeffery, visiting from Canada, presented Weightman with his Thermos. It still contained the coffee poured into it on April 23, 1945. Weightman was flabbergasted.

By early September, Dacon had slipped Moby Grip under NA337's wings and slowly brought the main section to the surface. It was then taken to the association's temporary operating base in Norway.

The Canadian Air Force sent a twelve-member team of engineers and technicians to disassemble the bomber. Canadian transport planes arrived to take crates containing the bomber to the Air Force Museum in Trenton, Ontario, located between Montreal and Toronto.

At Trenton, the Halifax Aircraft Association was ready to start the laborious task of restoring the aircraft. It appointed Bill Tytula as project manager. A retired lieutenant colonel who had experience in restoration, Tytula led a team of two hundred volunteers. They spent more than 300,000 hours working on the project.

One of the volunteers who worked in the machine shop was Lloyd Wright, a Halifax bomber pilot who flew thirty-three combat missions during the war.

Robert Wilson, Waterloo Region Record

NA337 shortly before it was unveiled at the Air Force Museum at Trenton, Ontario, in 2005.

Tytula and the volunteers wanted NA337 restored to the condition it was in before it sank in Lake Mjosa, before Flight Sergeant Weightman scrambled on to the dinghy, before Flight Lieutenant Alexander Turnbull called out "Dinghy! Dinghy! Ditch! Ditch!", before a bullet punctured the starboard wing, before it left Tarrant Rushton. They strived for perfection.

Many of the original parts were damaged, but the association obtained replacement parts from a variety of sources. A section of a rear fuselage came from Scotland where it was serving as a chicken coop.

When parts could not be obtained, the volunteers built them from the original plans.

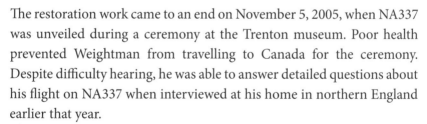

The restoration work came to an end on November 5, 2005, when NA337 was unveiled during a ceremony at the Trenton museum. Poor health prevented Weightman from travelling to Canada for the ceremony. Despite difficulty hearing, he was able to answer detailed questions about his flight on NA337 when interviewed at his home in northern England earlier that year.

Asked why he thought he was able to survive his ordeal in Lake Mjosa, Weightman chuckled and said it was because he was a "hardened Northumbrian."

He also handed over a few now-yellowing pages from a book, *Eclipse*, written in 1945 by war correspondent Alan Moorehead. They describe

Bill Darling

Thomas Weightman in 2005.

the bizarre flight to Oslo of the Dakota plane that freed Weightman. Moorehead happened to be one of the people aboard that flight.

Tore Marsoe, the Norwegian who heard the bomber, attended the Trenton ceremony. In a phone interview, during which he recounted his interest in the plane, he said he still remembered the throbbing sound of the bomber's engines.

Weightman, who died on September 3, 2007, never saw the restored bomber, but he knew it would serve as a classroom where young people could learn about the airmen who fought against Nazi Germany.

More than one hundred thousand people went to see NA337 during its first three years at the museum. They marvelled at the ruggedness of the plane and at the cramped quarters in which the men fought a long, horrible war. The aircraft reminds all who see it of the flyers who went off to war, both those who came home and those who didn't — and there were thousands who did not return. They lie in graves across Europe — in France, Belgium, the Netherlands, and Germany. The official history of the bombing campaign against Germany reports that 57,143 air force personnel from Commonwealth countries died during the war. This sombre statistic includes 9,980 members of the Royal Canadian Air Force. In addition, thousands were injured.

Historians may forever debate various aspects of the air war, but no one can ever doubt the courage of flyers such as Thomas Weightman and his crewmates on NA337.

BETWEEN THE LINES

They stood at attention, their uniforms pressed, their shoes polished, and their minds wandering to the skies over Europe. A band played a stirring march, such as "Captains of the Clouds." Every beat moved them closer to those skies. The airmen were at their wings parade.

When called individually, they marched to the commanding officer of their training base who would pin embroidered wings on them. The wings showed that the recipients were pilots, navigators, bomb-aimers, flight engineers, wireless operators, or gunners. This was their graduation day.

Today, we wouldn't call them men; we'd say they were teenage boys. Many were only eighteen. They had just learned to use a razor and now they were ready to use war machines designed to kill people and shatter cities.

Most never intended to be warriors in the air or anywhere else.

They wanted to be farmers, salespeople, bankers, or civil servants. They wanted peaceful jobs. They didn't want to go to war, but they feared Nazi Germany.

They were ready for the air force, but not necessarily ready for what they would experience while they served in it.

Collectively, they, along with millions of other airmen, soldiers, and sailors from the Allied countries, defeated Germany, but it took five and a half long years.

When they came home after the war, many veterans did not talk about what they had endured. Some were wounded; some lost limbs or an eye. Many had seen their friends die.

They knew that war may be necessary, but it isn't glorious. To some degree they were all wounded by the horror they had seen and the terror they had felt. For many, to talk about the war was to recall that horror, that terror. They wanted to be left to live their lives in peace, to raise their families, and to develop their careers.

Today, of course, the teenagers who were at those wings parades during the Second World War are in their eighties or nineties. When they attend a Remembrance Day service, they know they will see fewer comrades than the year before.

The passage of time will never erase what they saw and felt, but it has enabled many veterans to discuss their ordeals more easily with younger people — in many cases their children and grandchildren. They want young people to know what they experienced during the war.

We should know what they did, and we should express appreciation, but we should not just look at the veterans as if they are characters in a history book. The veterans have something to say to us about the future. They know that obstacles arise that are difficult to surmount, no matter when or where you live. They also know these obstacles will be different from the ones they faced — the type of challenges described in this book. The challenges young people face may be personal, educational, financial, or occupational.

Overcoming these challenges requires the same traits the airmen displayed: courage, initiative, determination — and some luck. This is the legacy presented to us by the survivors of the air war against Nazi Germany.

NOTES

CHAPTER 1: THE CAREER OFFICER

Because Keith Ogilvie died in 1998, I relied heavily upon his diary to describe how he attacked German planes and how they attacked him. His son, Keith Ogilvie Jr., provided me with a copy of the diary, as well as several published reports of battles in which his father participated. I also relied on 609 Squadron's operations records book, a copy of which was sent to me from England by Mark Crame.

I learned the details of Ogilvie's attack on the Dornier bomber from viewing film at the Imperial War Museum's film and video archive in London. The film came from a camera on Ogilvie's Spitfire.

Much of the information about Ogilvie's time in Stalag Luft III and his participation in the Great Escape came from an article, "Tigers in the Tunnel," that Ogilvie wrote in 1961 for an air force magazine, *The Roundel.*

Steve Martin, of the POW Archives of Canada, was particularly helpful in providing information about Stalag Luft III and the Great Escape. He gave me a copy of a report Ogilvie filed with the British intelligence agency MI9 after he returned to England.

Gord King, a prisoner at Stalag Luft III, offered details about the prison camp when a guard discovered the tunnel.

Ogilvie's wife, Irene, gave information about her husband's wartime experiences, as well as her own. Her daughter, Jean, assisted by asking questions on my behalf.

I learned about the incident in which Ogilvie obtained a guard's wallet by listening to an interview with him in a video documentary, *The Great Escape,* produced by Greystone Communications Inc.

Two books provided background on Ogilvie's participation in the escape, *The Great Escape* by Paul Brickhill, and *The Longest Tunnel* by Alan Burgess.

Philip LaGrandeur's book about RCAF prisoners of war and evaders, *We Flew, We Fell, We Lived,* also provided helpful information on the escape.

The Hurricane pilot who rammed the Dornier, Ray Holmes, described the attack in his book, *Sky Spy.*

CHAPTER 2: PATCHWORK

Clay Blair's book, *Hitler's U-Boat War: The Hunted, 1942–1945,* provided an interesting account of the attack on U-625 and the German navy's unsuccessful attempt to rescue the survivors.

CHAPTER 3: MARIA'S MEMORY

A commemorative booklet that Wilf Renner owns offered information about the Belgian Resistance. It describes the three parachute drops in which he participated.

CHAPTER 4: A FLIGHT FOR MALTA

Dan McCaffery's book, *Hell Island*, offered background on the siege of Malta and the island's strategic significance during the war.

CHAPTER 5: FINAL DESCENT

Harry Denison gave me several news articles written shortly after he returned to England. One was a transcript of an interview with Flight Lieutenant Bill Gill of the RCAF, conducted for the CBC.

CHAPTER SIX: THE GROUND WAR

John Wright, who knows George McHale, assisted by reading this chapter. William Arthur Bishop's book, *Destruction at Dawn*, provided details of the Luftwaffe raid known as Bodenplatte.

CHAPTER SEVEN: THE LUCKIEST GUY

Fred Greyer, in England, sent a copy of a British intelligence report on Carl Rudyk's crewmate, Albert Keveren. Oliver Clutton-Brock's book, *Footprints on the Sands of Time*, confirmed that Alfred Summers, another member of Rudyk's crew, became a prisoner of war.

CHAPTER EIGHT: THE CORPORAL'S RING

Rainer Kolbicz and Klaus-Peter Pohland helped me obtain a copy of U-96's log, which describes the submarine's attack on the *Anselm*. The original copy of the log is held by the National Archives and Records Administration in Maryland.

Anne and John Kroisenbrunner assisted by translating the log into English.

CHAPTER NINE: THE FOG OF WAR

A story in the *Daily Express* on April 24, 1942, supplemented Richard Gilman's recollection of the Battle for Freedom pageant.

The Torquay Reference Library in Torquay, England, assisted by providing details of the Luftwaffe raid on Torquay on June 7, 1942.

CHAPTER TEN: THE LAST TRAINING FLIGHT

Nona Collver, Ray Collver's daughter-in-law, relayed Collver's answers to questions I posed by email.

CHAPTER ELEVEN: A RIDE WITH FIFI

Bruno Beuken, son of Marietta Roemans, asked his mother on my behalf about the time Gordon Stacey spent with her family. Michael LeBlanc provided a copy of a report describing Mabel Fraipont's activities.

CHAPTER TWELVE: THE ESCORT

Dick Watson's daughter, Betty McGie, assembled news stories and documents about her father.

CHAPTER THIRTEEN: FLYING LESSONS

Ralph Campbell's book about his wartime experiences, *We Flew by Moonlight*, provided details of the two flights described in this chapter.

Ross McNeill supplied information from England about the RAF's search for Campbell's crew after they ditched in the English Channel.

CHAPTER FOURTEEN: THE LONG FALL

Rick Thomson offered information about Ben Marceau's ordeal. Thomson's mother's first husband, George Rowe, was the navigator on Marceau's crew.

Jim Hamilton provided background on the speed at which a person would fall to Earth.

CHAPTER FIFTEEN: THE LUCKY GUNNER

Mynarski's Lanc, a book compiled and edited by Bette Page, provided a full account of Pat Brophy's survival.

The 13th Mission, a CBC documentary report, contained interviews with several members of the crew, including Brophy.

André Coilliot gave background information on Brophy's time in France.

CHAPTER SIXTEEN: A STUDENT IN PARIS

Francois Cossard provided details about the Cossard family's farm.

Roy MacLaren's book, *Canadians Behind Enemy Lines, 1939–1945*, offered information on Robert Vanier and Yves le Hénaff.

CHAPTER SEVENTEEN: EAGLES AT WAR

The Last Escape, by John Nichol and Tony Rennell, provided an overview of the forced marches that moved prisoners away from the advancing Allied armies.

CHAPTER EIGHTEEN: THE SALUTE

Charles Brown wrote about his encounter with Franz Stigler in a chapter entitled, "Chivalry in the Clouds," in Martin W. Bowman and Theo Boiten's book, *Raiders of the Reich*.

Helga Stigler answered questions on behalf of her husband when poor health prevented him from doing so.

CHAPTER NINETEEN: A PLANE FOR TOMORROW

Jeff Jeffery, president of the Halifax Aircraft Association, and his wife, Elaine, provided background on the restoration of NA337, as did Bill Tytula, the project manager.

The statistics about bomber command's casualties came from *The Strategic Air Offensive Against Germany, 1939–1945, Volume IV*, by Sir Charles Webster and Noble Frankland.

ACKNOWLEDGEMENTS

This book isn't really my book. Dozens of people made contributions, both large and small. This book belongs to them as much as to me, because without their help I could not have written it. To all of them I will be forever grateful.

In particular, I want to acknowledge the veterans who spent hours patiently telling me what happened to them during the Second World War. I know many of them felt emotional pain when they described their ordeals. Time does not heal all wounds, particularly those caused by the loss of comrades.

I also want to thank the relatives of the veterans who provided information when the veterans had either died or were in poor health. Without them, I could not have completed some chapters. Their information kept the stories alive.

I want to thank one veteran in particular, Tom Lane, who is mentioned in the chapter entitled, "Eagles at War." Tom served as my "military adviser," scrupulously reading every chapter.

My family also offered wonderful assistance. My wife, Jane Ann, not only encouraged me during the six years I spent researching and writing these stories, but was my prime editor, always suggesting ways that each story could describe how the airmen felt, as well as what they did. My three daughters also helped. Amanda McLachlan Darling, along with her husband, John Recoskie, critiqued many of the chapters. Caroline McLachlan Darling, who works in museums, helped with research and photographs. My third daughter, Tamara Amirault, and her husband, Steve Amirault, resolved numerous computer problems. My father, Peter Darling, who is the subject of a chapter, "The Corporal's Ring," also read many chapters, and offered insights known to those who participated in the air war.

The newspaper where I work, the *Record* in Kitchener, helped in numerous ways. As well as offering support and encouragement, the paper published several of these stories. I also want to thank the *Toronto Star*, which belongs to the same newspaper chain as the *Record*. The *Star* ran condensed versions of stories. Whenever either the *Star* or the *Record* printed a story, I received numerous phone calls and email notes that offered information and assistance with this project.

Several members of the *Record*'s staff went beyond their regular tasks to help. Robert Wilson, the paper's senior photographer, offered tips on photographs. Robert, who has an interest in military history, also read the manuscript. Brenda Hoerle, an editor, assisted by reading several chapters, particularly the ones that mention members of the Royal Family. Steve Marshall, a systems analyst, helped me to arrange the manuscript in a format suitable for publication.

I would also like to thank Tony Hawke, editorial director of the Dundurn Group, which published this book. I will always appreciate the interest he took in these stories.

Meryl Keeling, a press officer at Buckingham Palace, helped me to obtain information about the Royal Family during the war.

ACKNOWLEDGEMENTS

Steve Martin of the POW Archives of Canada provided background, as well as comments for the chapters in which the veterans were prisoners of war.

Dr. David Waldbillig, chief of emergency medicine at Grand River and St. Mary's Hospitals in Kitchener, helped me to understand and describe some of the injuries that the veterans suffered.

Peter Devitt, assistant curator of the Royal Air Force Museum in London, provided information from the museum's archives.

Steve Jebson, information officer at the National Meteorological Library and Archive in Exeter, England, provided information about the weather on days when the veterans flew.

The Dominion Institute in Toronto helped me to contact several of the veterans.

Although I consulted numerous books, one was particularly useful, *The Bomber Command War Diaries* by Martin Middlebrook and Chris Everitt. It provided background for raids in which several of the veterans participated.

I fear that despite my best efforts I will have overlooked some people who helped with this book. To them, I offer both an apology and my appreciation.

INDEX

C

D

Dacon Sub Sea, 233, 234

Daddo-Langlois, Flight Lieutenant
Raoul, 63, 64, 67

Dardenne, Maria, 52–55, 57, 59, 60

Dardenne, Joseph Jr., 53, 54,

Darling, Warrant Officer George, 11,
203–206, 209, 212, 214

Darling, Corporal Peter, 96–105, 246

Davy, Marie-Madeleine, 195

de Breyne, Flying Officer Art, 180,
181, 183

Defence Ministry (Canadian), 176

de l'Ara, Sergeant Louis, 66

Delwaide, Jeanne, 136

Denison, Flight Sergeant Harry,
69–77, 241

Dodds, Sergeant Ted, 156, 157, 158,
160

Dugas, Sergeant Marcel, 189, 190, 200

Duke-Woolley, Squadron Leader
Raymond, 108

Dulag Luft, 87, 88,

Dulag Luft III, 73

Dumbarton, Scotland, 70

Dundalk, Ontario, 171

Dunn, Dr. Roger, 152

Durham, England, 156

Dutch Resistance, 18, 94, 127, 142

E

Eckenrode, Staff Sergeant Hugh, 217,
222, 223

Eden, Anthony, 32, 33, 35, 151

Edmonton, Alberta, 75, 83, 86, 91,
93, 94

Eisenhower, General Dwight, 136

Errey, Lance Corporal Donovan, 89

Essen, Germany, 169, 171, 173–175,
177

Etobicoke, Ontario, 122

Everett, Leading Aircraftman Dave,
99, 105

F

Fanuel, Dr. Robert, 49–52

Fare, Sergeant Arthur, 47, 48, 58

Felixstowe, England, 162, 167

Fengler, First Lieutenant Georg, 145

Fennell, Flying Officer Bob, 71, 75

Fern, Flight Lieutenant John, 170, 171

Foxboro, Ontario, 155, 166

Fraipont, Mabel (Fifi), 131–146

Frank, Captain Hans-Dieter, 206, 213

Frankfurt, Germany, 46, 47, 58, 73,
87, 187–189, 198, 201, 208, 209

Fraser, Sergeant Harry, 141

French Resistance, 130, 156, 157, 183,
184, 193, 195–199

Friday, Sergeant Jack, 181, 183,

Fuller, Sergeant Alan, 123, 127, 142,
144, 145

G

Galt (Cambridge), Ontario, 214

Gaunt, Pilot Officer Geoff, 18

Giles, Sergeant Ian, 70, 71, 76

Z

Of Related Interest

Dancing in the Sky

The Royal Flying Corps in Canada

C.W. Hunt

Dancing in the Sky
The Royal Flying Corps in Canada
by C.W. Hunt
978-1-55002-864-5 / $28.99

Dancing in the Sky is the first complete telling of the First World War fighter pilot-training initiative established by the British in response to losses occurring in European skies in 1916. It tells the story of the talented and courageous men and women who made the program a success, complete with the romance, tragedy, humour, and pathos that accompanies an account of such heroic proportions.

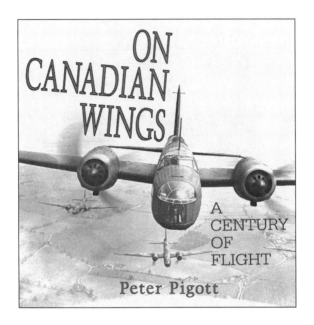

On Canadian Wings
A Century of Flight
by Peter Pigott
978-1-55002-549-1 / $49.99

Be prepared to soar! Whether you are an aviation enthusiast, history buff, or air traveller, don't miss these photo essays on aviation in Canada, covering almost 100 years of flight by Canadians. Dramatic visuals accompany each step of aviation's advances, from Canada's first military aircraft to Billy Bishop's Nieuport, from the earliest bush planes to the beginnings of passenger travel. This comprehensive history showcases 50 aircraft. Whether famous or forgotten, all were designed, built, and/or flown by Canadians.

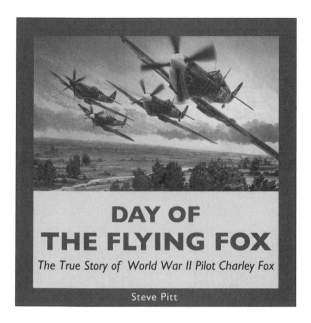

DAY OF THE FLYING FOX
The True Story of World War II Pilot Charley Fox

Steve Pitt

Day of the Flying Fox
The True Story of World War II Pilot Charley Fox
by Steve Pitt
978-1- 55002- 808-9 / $19.99

Canadian World War II pilot Charley Fox, now in his late eighties, has had a thrilling life, especially on the day in July 1944 in France when he spotted a black staff car, the kind usually employed to drive high-ranking Third Reich dignitaries. Already noted for his skill in dive-bombing and strafing the enemy, Fox went in to attack the automobile. As it turned out, the car contained famed German General Erwin Rommel, the Desert Fox, and Charley succeeded in wounding him.

Author Steve Pitt focuses on this seminal event in Charley Fox's life and in the war, but he also provides fascinating aspects of the period, including profiles of noted ace pilots Buzz Beurling and Billy Bishop, Jr., and Great Escape architect Walter Floody, as well as sidebars about Hurricanes, Spitfires, and Messerschmitts.

A Thousand Shall Fall
The True Story of a Canadian
Bomber Pilot in World War Two
by Murray Peden

978-1- 55002-454-8 / $27.99

During World War II, Canada trained tens of thousands of airmen under the British Commonwealth Air Training Plan. Those selected for Bomber Command operations went on to rain devastation upon the Third Reich in the great air battles over Europe, but their losses were high. German fighters and anti-aircraft guns took a terrifying toll. The chances of surviving a tour of duty as a bomber crew were almost nil.

 **DUNDURN PRESS**
www.dundurn.com

Available at your favourite bookseller

Tell us your story! What did you think of this book? Join the conversation at www.definingcanada.ca/tell-your-story by telling us what you think.